In loving memory of Mrs Klairi

KLAIRI
LYKIARDOPOULOU

*...and the
shadows
became
light*

MEGAS SEIRIOS
Publications

KLAIRI LYKIARDOPOULOU
...AND THE SHADOWS BECAME LIGHT
1st EDITION 2015

ISBN: 978-960-7350-95-4

This book is published by **Megas Seirios Publications**, founded by the **Servers' Society Spiritual Centre** based in Athens, Greece. To find more information about the mission, works and activities of the Society and/or to place an order, please visit our website:
www.megas-seirios.com

or contact us at:
9, Sarantaporou Street, Athens, Greece, P.O.: 111 44
e-mail: info@megas-seirios.com
Tel.: +30 210 20 15 194
Tel./Fax: +30 210 22 30 864

Translation from Greek: Dimitris Fragogiannis
Cover photo: Kostas Tzioumakas
Cover and book design: Marianna Smyrniotou

To the Masters
who teach the path of spiritual
evolution to humankind.

ও

CONTENTS

THE FIRST STEPS

We shall travel considerably back in time, to 1931, the previous century, and specifically to February of that year. It was then that I was born and the magical journey of my life began...

My parents were typical of the bourgeoisie of that time in Athens, where they permanently resided. Their economic prosperity permitted them to have a large apartment along with a maid. When I was born, they also hired a governess who followed my every footstep. My happy childhood was overshadowed only by her bawling and strong reprimands whenever I failed to meet her expectations, or was involved in mischief... You see, I was not always Mrs Klairi, nor was I directly born an adult.

Growing up, I began to notice and become aware of the world ever more clearly. Accompanied by an adult, as I was still young, I would walk the streets of the capital. There, outside the loving protection of my home, unfolded a world that was often shockingly mirrored in the eyes of my childhood naivety.

Greece was a poor country, and had barely recovered from the two Balkan wars, the First World War and the following Asia Minor disaster; conflicts that had taken place during only the last thirty years. Our daily lives, mine and my family's, were an exception which differed greatly from that of the majority of the population's, not only in the capital, but in the country in general. Luck had neglected to bless with its magic wand many of our fellow humans, who suffered, begging for a plate of food and some hope. But what this world was never at a loss for, was compassion. Others from their surplus and others from what little they had, helped by offering money or an edible commodity. All this could not easily fit into my child's mind. It seemed strange, and I wondered how there were people without even a roof, as we say, over their heads.

My parents travelled frequently. They liked getting to know other of our country's cities, as well as its islands. So, with time, they began taking me along. I particularly enjoyed our walks in the areas we visited. I observed the streets, the houses, the people, and gained my own images of the world that existed beyond the borders of my house's walls, and, in this case, the comfort of the hotel in which we lodged each time. And there, as in the capital, the same situation prevailed. Because something that this world never missed, was pain and misery. We returned to the hotel with legs tired from walking, accompanied by the thoughts of what we had seen. Sometimes beautiful and sometimes sad.

But in a faltering society, the first small cracks in my own safe environment were bound to appear sooner or later. I was playing in my parents' room that day, opening and closing drawers and cupboards, satisfying my curiosity for their contents and at the same time expressing my admiration for the beautiful clothes in them. My parents were there discussing, when I accidentally overheard a dialogue that, at the age of only four, caused me great concern over my family and myself.

"Your business has not been going well recently and my father is no longer able to financially support us, as he once used to", I heard my mother say. "I am not saying that we shall starve, but what if things get harder, if they get even more difficult?"

Her words, as expected for a girl of my age, greatly affected me. Upset, I sat still in front of the open closet and did not make a sound. I was terrified to even think about talking to them of my feelings. And in the years that followed, my mother's worried voice sounded many times in my ears, deterring me whenever I had to deal with financial matters. An example of how this event affected me, lurking for the opportunity to manifest at any time, is when I started working as a kindergarten teacher. A colleague suggested we open our own school, but I immediately refused without a second thought. I did not want to assume any financial responsibility or risk whatsoever. Similarly, when I got married, I entrusted my husband with my entire salary for him to manage, keeping only what was necessary each time.

And the years passed... Almost ten years after my birth, the longsuffering Greece found itself under German occupation. The dark clouds of World War II had thickened over Europe. The destructive fury of this war left no one unaffected. But what cost me most was the death of one my uncles, who was killed by a gunshot during a scuffle with the invaders. I was very fond of him, as he told me of things still unknown to me, enriching my knowledge and sharpening my perception. After his death and for many years, I kept a picture of him by my bed so as to remember him.

A further disruption arising because of the occupation, was the closing down of the private school I had been attending. Both my classmates and I continued our courses at another school which was quite far from our homes. But these problems were certainly meaningless compared to the despair many people faced, lacking the basics and not knowing if they would have food in the morrow. Naturally, the era of prosperity in our home had passed, and not a day went by that I did not agonize until ascertaining that what I saw on the table was enough for everyone.

Eventually the shadow of occupation withdrew, leaving behind it, however, deep wounds and pain. But the relief for the end of the war was great and the seed of hope that the lives of all would finally change for the better began to grow. And the prayer of all, myself included, was that our hopes became a reality. The curfew after sunset imposed by the Germans ceased. So did a whole lot of other prohibitions, such as the illumination of houses at night. The state would be rebuilt again and, even at a slow pace, people would find work again, just as my father soon did. Things, of course, continued to be difficult. And a few days later, our hopes would be belied by the outbreak of the December Events. On the streets, where a few days before people exclaimed "Christ is Risen", embracing each other, they now tore each other to pieces, pointing the barrels of their weapons against one another.

My father was often strict with me, wanting to point out my mistakes. My mother, on the other hand, though more rarely, blamed me for errors which I did not feel were my own fault. These behaviours however never made me reconsider the love I received from both of them.

At that time, I started making friends with the neigh-bours. We gathered at the home of one or the other, or played out in the streets. The cars back then were few. Nowadays things are very different. Our parents were not concerned about leaving us alone out in the neighbour-hood. Nevertheless, the company of my friends was not offset by my desire to acquire a sibling to play with, a wish that was belatedly fulfilled.

My sister was born when I was six and a half years old. I was amused with her funny faces and rocking movements while she was a baby. For a short time only, I played with her after returning from school. But this happened more and more sparsely, because, as she grew, naturally I grew too, and so did my increasing obligations for study.

But I was not only older than my sister – I was the old-est of all our cousins, who were numerous, considering the fact that my father had seven siblings. And, I must admit, I was quite proud of it. On the side of my father, my grandfather had died a few weeks before I was born, while my grandmother had undertaken the task to con-vey to her grandchildren her faith and her love for reli-gion, just as she had done with her own children.

We frequently exchanged visits to the homes of our relatives. The same happened with my mother's parents, who lived near our home and visited us on an almost dai-ly basis. My grandfather was a generous man who often brought me toys. But even when there was no toy for him to give me, he would place me in a game process akin to a treasure hunt. When I was not looking, he would hide some money in the armchair where he sat or somewhere else and would reveal it to me with a broad smile before our farewell, saying that it was my job was to discover its hiding place. Before our final farewell, the last and only thing he said was: "Take care of the children." Since then, I never again recovered money hidden in armchairs or behind ornaments, unless they had fallen out of our pockets.

After the death of her husband, my grandmother came to stay with us. She was a religious woman that had also dealt with esotericism. She had started indulging in theosophy after a trip with her daughters to Switzerland when she was younger. There, she had met some people who had respectively recommended theosophy to her. The door to her room was often closed, as she wished to relax and study. She devoted plenty of time reading relevant books and, depending on my age, conveyed to me certain elements of her knowledge. Her interest in others, and especially in her grandchildren, was evident, responding whenever one of us had a problem.

I remember when I was about nine years old, she had asked me if I wanted to accompany her to Amerikis Square. Her proposal delighted me, as it had already been a year since the occupation, and we avoided walking on the streets or footling because of the constant fear of an unexpected incident that would jeopardize our lives. We only went out when and if there was a specific need. My joy for our walk soon though turned into unspeakable grief. Two children, a little older than me with bellies swollen from hunger begged for some food. But, at that time, who had anything to give? Nevertheless, to the extent that anyone could, and going above and beyond, people responded to others' needs, as indeed, did we. And so, they moved away saddened, just as we did.

However, the sight that awaited me at Amerikis Square made me burst into tears. From the branches of a tree hanged two lifeless bodies. Who they were, who had hanged them and why, was of little importance to me right then. And even if my grandmother had given me some explanation, in my agitation I certainly could not remember. The only thing I managed to hold on to from her words was her reference to the inhumanity and violence, something that gave me no comfort. On the contrary, it made me cry even harder. I started walking towards our home, seeking its safe embrace. My grandmother followed me, and when she finally caught up with me, she continued to explain:

"You have now grown up. You cannot avoid evil. Nor is it enough for me to speak to you only of people's kindness, as I have done up to now. In the world you will meet

16

violence, malice and abhorrence. But you need not fear evil, nor those who act so. When you become an adult, you will have to deal with it. So, since this happened, it is best to know of it from now on. So that you can start thinking, perceiving. You have to explain to others where the problem is and tell them what they need in order to change their attitude.

You know, the ones who hanged them were no good. But those who were hanged were no better. They were black marketers. Coming here, you saw with your own eyes the children suffering. Yet, these people endured leaving them so, to their fate, profiteering against those who suffer and are in need. I do not judge what punishment is appropriate or not, or if they deserved what happened to them, but what you saw remains an example of what happens to those who are indifferent to their fellow humans."

Indeed, that year alone, and only in Athens and Piraeus, an estimated one thousand souls died every day of malnutrition. And so, although it was hard on behalf of my grandmother and hard for me to accept or even to understand what she had told me, it did not cease to be a reality. A reality which not only would I have to deal with while growing up, but I would also need to understand its underlying causes. And, however strange it may sound, to admit their existence even within me, to accept and to change them!

ADOLESCENT CONCERNS

In winter, when evening fell, my father would light a brazier in one of the rooms. There, we would all gather around the fire to keep warm. The cosiness of the warmth as well as that of the family's, was certainly pleasant. But not for long...

Once I began entering my adolescence, I expressed the need, as was natural, to stay for hours by myself in my room. So, eventually, this mandatory family gathering began to displease me. And I say *mandatory* because due to the cold we avoided moving away from the one and only brazier that warmed the space around it. My father, wanting to save money, stubbornly refused to turn on the heater and warm up the whole house, contrary to my constant appeals. My parents tried coaxing me, but I sought my isolation, something that in time started influencing me in a negative way.

Additionally, puberty brought with it a greater preoccupation with my body and a concern over my form. Like any young person, I too wanted to be liked, to have an acceptable, not only character, but also face and body. That was when I began to notice and pay attention to my legs, and particularly my calves that were visibly thicker than normal, a trait I inherited from my mother. My father, perceiving my discomfort caused by the disproportionate to the rest of my body calves, advised me to cover them by wearing longer skirts. Despite his mistaken approach, which hurt me at the time, I followed his advice and tried to hide my legs from the eyes of others and particularly those of my peers. Especially after an incident at the beach...

That summer day I was taking a dip in the sea, when I heard two young men commenting on my legs, referring to my calves as inelegant. That equally inelegant comment affected me so much that I wrapped myself in my towel and put an end to my swim. Since then, I did everything in my power to avoid giving a handle to people commenting on my body.

Unfortunately, adolescence lasts for a while and the problems that accompany it appear as soaring mountains. The elements of a personality are asserted and often views are expressed which we consider unable to manage or to live with. This also happened to me. I struggled with my contradictions; on the one hand I wanted to appear great and on the other I could not bear any imperfection of my body or any weakness of my character. And, as expected, this was a catalyst for many major conflicting situations within me, as well as with those who I socialized with. At the slightest criticism from others or even from myself, even on matters which I had admitted and confessed to myself – such as my thick calves and my displeasure over them – I was saddened, reacting strongly. And then, all the negative comments that I had at times heard from my family or friends, would flare up.

On the other hand, I felt validated when the expressions of others were positive towards me. There were people who sought my company, who enjoyed chatting with me and often confessed their problems to me and trusted my judgment. I remember, for example, that an acquaintance of mine had asked for my advice on her relationship with her boyfriend, as things were not going well between them. After much thought, I told her my opinion and I added that if their relationship did not eventually improve, there was always the option of separation. She was reluctant to do so, despite agreeing with me. So during the following days, whenever we met, I stubbornly repeated the same thing to her, wanting to provoke a response. But she did nothing whatsoever. Irrespective of her own attitude and without considering whether mine was correct or not, I admired the trust she showed to me. I considered that I was very important and was deluded by the idea that because of my importance, the people around me sought my company. I did not realize that exactly what I thought of myself urged me to confront others in a way that eventually pushed them away from me.

This became particularly evident when a good friend explained to me that I was out of line towards a relative of mine and that, moreover, in his opinion, what I had said to her was wrong. I was so angry at him that, after an intense argument, I left, determined not to speak to him again. My attitude persisted for a long time and led to such a disaffection on his side, that he eventually discontinued any communication with me. Only then did I begin thinking that maybe all that he had told me was right, or, additionally, that I might be wrong in the way I behaved towards him, as well as towards my relative. It was one of the few times that I admitted and confessed to myself that I was utterly wrong. Thus, I decided to the approach him again and to apologize. But as I said, this was merely an exception at that time.

There were two things that I enjoyed, dancing and swimming. Indeed, my desire for them was so great that I was unconcerned whether they led me to unwillingly show off my legs. When I danced or swam I felt wonderful, I felt free, and, magically, my obsession to appear great weakened, as was the case with my grief for my unshapely body, which was momentarily forgotten. Curiously, I would then became more receptive to the criticism of others. Especially when they were experts in dancing or swimming. When someone pointed out the mistakes in my movements and corrected me, I immediately did whatever I could to improve myself, listening carefully and without resistance. When I one day asked a dance teacher why this happened, he answered me directly.

"When you surrender yourself without inhibitions in order to express yourself through dancing, and experience within you the freedom these movements offer you, why should there be a desire to appear great? Or why should you be concerned about accepting your ignorance in any other issue? When you dance you are absorbed in it one hundred percent, and when you place your whole self into what you do, what you project emerges from the clear depth of your being where there is no room for personality needs or resistances against a difficulty."

I must confess, I had rarely received such answers in my life until then. It was obvious that this particular person had this answer exactly because it was experienced through his adoration of dancing. Extrapolating his own thought, I realized that the same happened to me when

I was swimming. In the beneficial embrace of nature, within the cool waters of the sea, I felt free, free from restricting thoughts. But, of course, I could not constantly dance or swim. And, certainly, the feeling I had in these activities was one I was unable to expand and experience throughout the rest of my day, where I continued hiding my legs and wanting to appear great.

Something that also got me thinking after that conversation, was that I started mistakenly believing that my adulthood would bring about it the resolve of many of my problems. If the dance teacher, being an adult, had such a vision and attitude for life, obviously I too had to have patience until I grew up and reached the same understanding... of an adult! I naively thought that along with my coming of age qualifying me for any legal transaction and the acquisition of voting rights, maturity would also come. Clearly, I saw around me mostly adults with adolescent behaviour, but it was not what I thought, or wanted to think of myself. And it was reasonable to wonder whether that which we ultimately ignore is our coming of age and its effective realization.

Of course, adolescence did not fail to bring with it a disturbance in matters of love. Besides, how could I ignore the need to look great or beautiful, which was necessarily and primarily associated with this issue? Nevertheless, I maintained an indifferent attitude even towards those of my peers who showed an interest in me and wished to initiate a relationship. I often thought about the cause of my indifference, but always ended up leaving things as they were until the appearance of a suitable young man who would satisfy my rather strict criteria and provide me with what I required.

Obviously, I have mentioned my adolescence quite briefly, but I do not doubt that the confusion of that age is something that everyone, in one way or another, has gone through and experienced. So, as I did not understand much of what was happening to me, I was content in the complacency of my wishful thinking that sooner or later I would become an adult and most things inside me would be clarified...

COMING OF AGE

When the period of occupation ended I was thirteen years old, still in the early stages of adolescence. My parents, and especially my father, decided to enrol me in the *American College for Girls* in order to also learn the English language. At the time, the College was located in the area of Elliniko, where I went with the school bus. That was in fact the reason why my mother was not sure about this choice; that is, to go every day to a school that was so many kilometres away from our house. She worried about my safety in case of a car crash, but my father was reassuring and finally convinced her that there was no reason to worry. Besides, his argument was unshakeable, since, as I have already mentioned, the cars on the streets at the time were very few. My mother's agitation, though justified, was unfounded, as has been proved. We never faced any problems on the way to school. On the contrary, the drive with my classmates was very pleasant, especially when we reached the sea on the coastal road.

By the end of my first school year there, a teacher suggested I become class president on the following year. I was surprised because I had in mind that the position would be proposed to a classmate of mine that had already attended that school all the previous years. But since things were so, I gladly accepted. When I was going through the penultimate year of my education at school, there was one more suggestion from my teachers. This time it was that I should undertake the self-government of all the presidents from all classes of the school. They did not request my immediate answer. Besides, it was still very early, just after the opening of the school following the Christmas holidays. Still, I announced my decision to them very soon – I wanted to do it.

The next year, however, something unpleasant happened during an exam. As I had not studied sufficiently, I secretly kept some notes, the so-called cheat-sheets I assume everyone is familiar with, and whenever the teacher looked away I consulted them. But luck was not on my side. The teacher caught me and I suffered her sharp reprimand, telling me that what I did was forbidden and unacceptable; especially on my part as I had undertaken the management of the presidencies of classes. After the rest of the teachers were informed of my venture, they decided I should no longer be in charge of the presidencies. Apart from humiliation, my grief was so great that I thought I would never get over it.

Nevertheless, the passing of time acted as a cure. Although my grief did not cease to exist, at least it was considerably reduced. On the exams for my diploma, the grades I got were very good, so I decided to continue attending extra lessons relating to my career orientation. I completed my registration in the relevant department which I considered the most appropriate, without encountering any opposition from my parents. They rarely disagreed with my decisions, unless they found them completely wrong. Besides, when I finished school I was already eighteen years old and this was an advantage in order to more easily express my views and choices. Of course, at that time, the long awaited coming of age was typically after twenty-one, but, really, who had the patience to wait... Like any young person, I had my whole life ahead of me and I wanted to live it.

My plans also included traveling, this time not with my parents but with my friends. So, during the holiday season we visited many different parts of our country. And my impressions were always the same. Aside from my admiration for the natural beauty of our country, the mountains, the plains, and the seas, we mostly encountered poor households and non-existent public works. The contrast with what I saw when I eventually started traveling to other European countries was enormous. The prosperity of these countries and the exploitation of their wealth was reflected not only in their homes but also in the luxurious hotels, the fabulous cars, the public places, on every step we made in the cities or even in the countryside. I was enchanted, momentarily forgetting the difficulties that existed back home. But when we returned again, soon and even more painfully, I noticed the poverty that the largest part of the population suffered.

Completing my studies in college, I worked as a clerk in the office of one of my uncles. One day, after work and on the way home, I ran into a family friend in a cafe. I sat down with him to exchange news, but the discussion expanded and he mentioned a Greek-American association that in its diverse activities included scholarship loans for US universities. I immediately started collecting letters of recommendation and whatever else was necessary to join this program. Gradually, the letters started arriving at our house. I was eager to gather as many as I needed and when most were in my hands, I proceeded to fill out the application. I had but to wait for their answer...

I did not know when I would have an answer and I was uncertain of whether it would be positive. I had decided to become a kindergarten teacher. Not only for the simple initial knowledge I believed I could convey to young children, but above all because I cared about them and wished for their well-being.

The answer finally arrived and it was positive. Overjoyed, I packed my suitcases and immediately began my journey, always with the consent of my parents. The day after my arrival in New York, I found myself in the *University of North Carolina*, impressed by all I had seen during my trip through this unknown to me and prosperous country. When I arrived I was greeted with a pleasant and warm welcome from the association members who had undertaken my scholarship, and later by my fellow students.

Throughout my stay there, I rarely felt displeasure. But whenever I did, I realized that I was missing something, but I did not know what. I was very satisfied with my studies, as the teaching that I received was consistent with the views I had on how to care for young children. The teachers were not limited to a sterile transfer of knowledge on what and how a kindergarten teacher must be. They expanded on issues more substantial relating to how each child can properly develop as well as the contribution of the family, the environment in general, in its shaping. When I eventually worked as a kindergarten teacher, I got to implement these skills. However, there were many times when I had to look up my university books and consult them when I was faced with cases I did not know how to respond to.

My student life went by smoothly and pleasantly. I had a good relationship with everyone, and both teachers and fellow students dealt with me positively and sympathetically. Indeed, the motion on the part of the Greek-American association to provide a six-month extension on my scholarship deeply moved me. When the time came to go back home, after receiving my diploma, my university had one last surprise for me; a farewell celebration, where I had the opportunity to thank my teachers and the people I had met there.

I arrived in Athens on March 1953, in the early post-civil war period, and the outlook seemed quite positive. I was now an adult!

WORKING WOMAN

The first issue I wanted to address upon returning home was finding a job on my specialty as a kindergarten teacher. As we were in the middle of the school year, I had plenty of time ahead of me to research and to send my resume.

After several visits to schools, I found it most suitable to work in a nursery of a well-known private school. At the meeting with its principal, I informed him of my professional training and work competence and I got the job. I worked there until my early retirement, with a four-year break after the first two years. As it was the first time I worked as a kindergarten teacher, I often had to observe my colleagues and learn from them, until I gained some experience of my own. Despite all my studies and what I had been taught, my knowledge still did not seem satisfactory in practice. Meeting the needs of children of this age was not easy. Even after several years I continued to learn about how to respond better to them. And even when I had gained considerable experience, there were always cases requiring a more particular approach and greater engagement.

Throughout my professional course I became an observer of children. I watched their reactions, and whether they accepted or rejected the way in which I approached them. Many times their behaviour was a direct result of their family environment and that was something I could easily perceive, as we had a meeting with the parents every fortnight, at least with those able to or who did not avoid contact with the kindergarten teachers.

I had the tendency to observe all people with whom I was surrounded, even those I met on the street. This was something I had done since I was a child, as I imagine is the case with most children. But my findings now greatly differed from those I had as a child. What I mostly discerned in adults was a behaviour often befitting an adolescent, and certainly not a person of their age. I was particularly troubled with this finding, as I was with the immaturity I often expressed myself.

I was beginning to wonder about this formal adulthood that the government stipulated as coming on our twenty-first year of age. But the transition from one age to another signified absolutely nothing. Although an adult now, my longing to operate as a real adult had not been fulfilled. I continued to wonder who was able to lead us to our effective adulthood and if indeed this could actually be achieved. In any case, books and knowledge were certainly not a guiding principle for it.

Then, among the kindergarten children, I first thought that whoever had the answer for our coming of age must definitely have realized it for him or herself. And soon I wondered if that person might be able to aid us in the corresponding realizations we were called to do.

THE TWO SIDES
OF MARRIED LIFE

The acquaintance with my husband arose, as was common at the time, by our parents' desire to meet each other. An acquaintance which they believed might likely lead to marriage, as indeed happened.

We met in a café, and I immediately noticed that our gazes scanned each other's form. This was of course expected; mainly because we operate so in all our interactions, as the first attraction or repulsion we feel about someone is relevant to their form. We sat down, ordered and started chatting. Unlike him, who did not seem to pay any attention to my legs, a matter which still remained troubling for me, I was indeed bothered by bandage of a temporary wound on one of his fingers. Instantly realizing that this was completely absurd, I stopped fixating on it.

The conversation led us to the trips he made as a representative of the company he worked for. He had stayed three years in India and the next two in Baghdad, Iraq, where he had to return to the following month. I barely knew anything of what he told me about these countries, contrary to him, who was hardly unaware of what I told him of my own trips and especially the one to the United States. We decided to meet again the next day, and then the day after that and so on, until we ended up seeing each other every day.

On a trip to his hometown, Volos, in order to settle some issues for his work, I accompanied him. We enjoyed the snow in the surrounding mountains and our pleasure slowly started turning into love.

The days he would be remaining in Athens were few. I was troubled by the thought of following him to Baghdad, since I would be forced to leave my kindergarten position in the middle of the year. On the other hand, we were not happy with the thought of extending our wedding date until he returned home. So we decided to talk to the kindergarten principal about resolving the issue of my absence there. My employer agreed for me to hand over my class's children to a trainee kindergarten teacher and wished me a quick return so that I could to go back to my position again. Something which in fact happened four years later!

Preparations for our wedding began after only three and a half weeks of acquaintance between us. We rushed to book a church, to find a best man and to take care of all the relevant details. In fact, with us, at the same time and in the same church, his brother also got married, which brought even more joy to our families. And three days after our wedding we left for Baghdad...

From Athens we reached Cyprus by boat, and then Beirut, from where we continued by bus to Baghdad. During our journey I asked my husband, who had completed this trip many times, about everything that I saw for the first time.

In the early days, and until we found a permanent home in Baghdad, we lodged in a hotel. Soon a house was found, and the necessary work began in order to transform it into our new home. Of course, having grown up in the comforts of our family home, where my mother with the help of our maid dealt with the cleaning, tidying up, cooking and generally all the care and daily household chores in their entirety, I was totally inexperienced in my new role. Nevertheless, I was confident that I could manage just fine. Until one day I had to cook dinner for some of our friends who were coming over...

I made plenty of food and took care of our guests. But during dinner I noticed with regret that our diners very discreetly counted each mouthful and politely refused more food servings, saying that they were full as an excuse. I very much wanted to believe it, but when our guests left, my husband, to my great disappointment, confirmed my suspicions. The potatoes were hard, almost raw, while the rest of the food was tasteless. Since then, and for some time, I became completely helpless as to cooking and every time I would take the advice of my husband who, as having lived alone for a long time, was a relatively better cook than I was.

But what really brought us into conflict with each other was the driving lessons he was trying to give me. He believed that I had to know exactly how a car engine worked, while I only cared about being simply its operator, using it only for my tasks and outings. It would suffice to teach me to be a good driver and to be able to change a flat tire if need be. Our disagreement culminated every time I sat in front of the wheel and we each insisted strongly on our own view. In the end, we decided to stop talking about this issue even when we thought about it. This of course did not actually solve the problem, since we both grumbled within.

To this day I have kept many of our photographs from those times; mementos of happy moments, with us laughing, singing and discussing about various pleasant subjects. However, this country was not the most welcoming, at least relating to living conditions. I remember that one night, as we were lying down, we saw above us a spider coming down from the ceiling. Really, someone would reasonably ask, you were afraid of a spider? But let us not overlook the fact that this spider had a deadly sting. Luckily, my husband took action, removing it and killing it.

The climate there was also very unpleasant and, as I was told by a doctor, it was best for Europeans who were unaccustomed to it, not to stay there too long, especially women. Shortly before the birth of our second child, our eldest daughter and I returned by plane to Greece. Another reason that had contributed to this decision was the recommendation of my gynaecologist, for the care I should take regarding the health of both myself and the foetus. My husband remained there to deal with some pending issues relating to his job.

Three days after we returned to Greece, we were informed by radio of the overthrow and murder of King Faisal in Iraq and the ban on exiting the country. It was July 1958. I greatly agonized about what could happen to my husband. A few days later I received a telegram from him saying only that he was well. This reassured me and our relatives, but the agony on when he would manage to come back to us did not stop until he returned to Athens, indeed before I gave birth and the christening of our first daughter.

Our married life continued with all its ups and downs in the home we set up in Greece. Of all the things my husband did, what I really could not tolerate was the fact that whatever he tackled, it absorbed him almost completely, wasting too much of his time. Despite his good intentions and despite my admiration for the dedication he showed in whatever he did, I especially fret that he was able to spend night and day trying, for example, to find a solution to an issue in our house, such as a problem which might have appeared with the electric circuit. I felt that because of this attitude he neglected both myself and the children, who at the time might possibly be wanting his attention or had some other need. I often talked to him about this issue, but he did not understand me and I was not able to accept this function of his. So once again, I ended up not dealing with something that bothered me, leaving it unresolved and pretending not to notice it. But in this way, the only thing I managed was to create grey areas in my marriage and in my relationship with my husband.

Of course, all married couples face difficulties similar to our own; difficulties often caused by something that at a distance might look small and funny, but is enough to torpedo our relationship and force us to shut ourselves out. Differences, difficulties and tensions between a married couple are expected. But either way we choose to solve our problems, that is either with indifference or with continuous friction – in both cases with each party insisting on its own correctness – we do not achieve anything. We only cause the stagnation of an uncomfortable situation for everyone. So it was only fitting at that time to wonder if there is a better way to resolve these situations, which although I did not understand why, seemed inevitable.

The complaints, feelings of unfulfillment and questions raised, along with the joys and cuddles that were not lacking, once again reminded me of my incompetence. As from time to time happened in my student years, so now did I realize that I would have to ask for the missing piece in the puzzle of life and relationships. But, much as I expected, this fulfillment did not come. On the contrary, sometimes I felt that my knowledge, instead of increasing, diminished. No matter how much I told myself to let things run smoothly without my own continuous interventions and to trust that everything would happen as it should, the doubts, the inhibitions and the reactions were ubiquitous, leaving me inconsolable.

FAMILY LIFE

I continued to be impressed by my husband's beautiful descriptions of the various parts of the world he visited. He still travelled, and on the summer months when I had the opportunity, I went with him. But that was not the only thing that impressed me about him...

His interest in new technology and machines was great. That was the reason why when the first televisions appeared in Greece, he rushed to buy one. In our house you could find everything, from the most sophisticated cameras of the time, to wireless radios and telescopes. Some of these absorbed him enough that he dabbled with them for hours, leaving a trail of components and cables throughout various rooms of the house. The interest he had for machines, he equally showed for history knowledge, always trying to be aware of current world affairs. In fact, our visitors often turned into a welcoming audience for him.

Time passed and we had a son, our third child. As he was born in the summer, I did not have to stop my work at the kindergarten, where I went with our daughters. In the mornings when I was away at work, the custody and care of our son was in the hands of my mother, with the help of a maid. As the children grew, we watched them with pleasure trying to slowly do things for themselves, such as turning the television on and off, watering the pot plants, or placing on a gramophone plate – as we called vinyl records at the time. Not wanting to discourage them, we refrained from correcting them if they did something wrong. We let them figure the right way out for themselves and laughed when our first daughter exclaimed: "By myself, by myself!"

Their father often bought them toys, which made them very happy. When he brought them home, they spread them all in one room. Most often they required plenty of space as they consisted of various constructions which he took care to explain how to assemble. They could be engaged for days with each toy, together with his own help. But gradually they would lose their interest and get bored. On the contrary, the only one continuing undeterred until the constructions' completion, was my husband. My children and I all gazed at him and laughed at his antics, until one of us would finally decide to go and help him.

During her adolescence, our eldest daughter faced an eating disorder. She ate little and with difficulty, something that gave us great concern. We had heard that a disorder such as anorexia can occur at these ages, but we certainly did not know how to deal with it. In order to help as best we could, we invited friends to our home or went out to taverns, in the hope that the pleasant surroundings would make her relax and eat with greater ease. A long time passed until this situation finally reached an equilibrium. And this experience definitely bequeathed us concern for our other children when they too would enter adolescence.

However, with our second daughter there were other issues we had to deal with. In her adolescence she began to react strongly to whatever we said, with these conflicts lasting until she grew up and started her own family. Our son, on the other hand, had no particular reactions towards us, but had inherited from his father the almost obsessive insistence in being absorbed for a long time with whatever he addressed. I did the same with my son as I had been doing with my husband, remaining uninvolved in this behaviour.

Having a family, in addition to the difficulties arising each time, did not bring me the completeness I had
expected. I did not give my husband the satisfaction he
sought; instead, I wished to receive it from him. Even
when I made the decision to function differently, it did
not last for long and I soon went back to earlier behaviours. Similar decisions of mine were also unstable with
the other members of my family and there were times
when I wondered if love alone suffices. But this love on
my part was not expressed consistently as it was overshadowed by anger and frustrations. Result of this unstable position on love along with the denial to offer – for
whatever reasons – what the other person really asks,
was the continual rise and fall, depending on the events
and the corresponding emotional state each time.

We all have examples of such attitudes both within
and outside our family circle. There are times when we
operate directly and with simplicity, without thinking
about it too much, and then the situations take a different course than expected. As happened with my husband and I when, without him knowing it, I gave an ex-
pensive vase to a friend of mine. She was facing financial
difficulties at the time and was in great need of money,
so she sold it. Despite the fight I was sure to follow when
my husband found out, when I eventually told him, he
hugged me and said that he considered it more important that I did not conceal it and showed trust in him.

His work and responsibilities, however, did not often leave him the margin to be equally effusive. Many times he would return home tired, tense or angry. That period he would often come into conflict with a partner of his and this greatly charged him. One afternoon after work, as he was relaxing in the armchair without doing anything, I approached him and turned on the radio. I knew the cause of his fatigue and did not care to attribute responsibilities or decide who was right and who was wrong. Looking at him with a smile, I started quietly singing the song playing on the radio at that moment, as if dedicating it to him. His mood gradually changed and he came to me, accompanying my singing.

But if ultimately things could flow so simple that each party responds to the need of the other, why did we not do so often or even always? Instead, we remain in difficulty, ultimately fuelling it and expanding it.

The tensions, quarrels, and resistances that I had with my husband or with my children, which could often become painful, were due to our differences. But these differences were not necessarily negative. It was up to us to cross check them so that they were utilized towards the interests of us all, for the further union between us. But this, at the time, was only big talk and theories...

CALLING FOR A DIFFERENT COURSE

As our two daughters progressed into their adolescence, they ceased desiring, as expected, to accompany us to the vacation home we had near Corinth. They preferred to stay in Athens with their friends or go on excursions with them. Our son, who was the youngest in age and therefore continued to come with us to the countryside, was left alone. So we often called his friends to come to our home for the summer vacations while he also began looking for new friends from the neighbourhood. But as his own adolescence progressed, he began arranging his own schedule during the holiday season, as his sisters had already been doing.

Despite the fact that everyday obligations relating to the care of our children had dwindled, when we returned to Athens and I went back to my work, I still felt great fatigue. I had already been a kindergarten teacher for several years and so I thought that maybe it was due to this accumulation. However, within me I realized that such an explanation was nothing but an excuse. Something else was to blame, which I was not aware of. I wondered again about what was happening to me and from whom I would receive the answer I was searching for.

The school principal noticed my weariness and offered to discuss the issue with me in order to find a solution. He suggested I did not to take on an entire class but to only have specific responsibilities, such as painting and playing with clay. The understanding he exhibited and his facilitation was comforting. The reduced responsibilities would help me not to tire so, although I never stopped thinking about the possibility of an early retirement. If I decided so, it had to be done before my son completed his eighteenth year of age when he would be considered an adult, as the law now dictated. I had less than a year ahead of me to make my decision and initiate the necessary procedures.

Despite the new conditions in my work, which were not as demanding as before, my fatigue persisted, so I proceeded to announce to my employer that I would soon withdraw from my work. After contacting the relevant social security office, I confirmed that the earliest I was entitled to retire, having a minor child, was at the age of fifty. And so it happened.

At that time my husband often travelled abroad for business. The children had their own occupations and, as they had now grown up, they were usually gone for several hours from home. I enjoyed the quiet and their absence allowed me to occupy myself with whatever I liked, such as knitting and embroidery. I also started painting again. I hadn't dealt with painting since I was a child. My father felt that I did not have the corresponding talent and since then I had given up, excluding very rare instances. Now that I was alone for many hours, I found myself painting more and more often. In fact, I was very pleased when our first daughter, who had from a young age shown an inclination to painting, decided to study at the *School of Fine Arts*. I remember that when we walked on the street, she would observe and comment on the colours and shadings on the clothes of passers-by. Later, at home, she would try to capture the colours and shapes on paper, clumsily still due to her age. And in primary school, the margins in her notebooks were decorated with various sketches that she made during class.

Unanswered questions flooded me from when I was still a child. Questions that as I grew developed into existential concerns, to which was added the need for solutions to everyday problems and difficulties. This whole tangled mess inside of me urged me to seek someone whom I considered more of an expert than myself to ask for advice. The thought of visiting a psychiatrist wandered for a while in my mind. At that time, I saw this as the only option I had. I discussed it with my husband, and, without hesitation, he agreed with me and supported me in my decision. He knew that I desperately sought to validate that something else, deeper and more meaningful, was the reason, the purpose of our existence, of our birth. He also knew that my unanswered quest was making me so tired that I could respond neither to his needs nor to our children's. And this led them to similar behaviours towards me.

Asking certain of our acquaintances whose judgment I trusted, I finally arrived at a psychiatrist whom I considered the most appropriate. In our meetings, I explained my problems and my concerns, which ultimately had little relation to the difficulties in my family, my relationships with others or the best I could do about them. I mostly, if not mainly, focused on my own function within life itself. Even if my quest was intense or not, or influenced me often or rarely, the fact that it continued to exist tortured me. I believed that he, the psychiatrist, would have solutions and answers to my problems.

At first the visits were frequent, but after three months they started to thin. I did not feel satisfied or covered at all but, as it turned out, neither was he, as I was not the easiest person he had met in his career. When one day he told me something that greatly disturbed me, I decided that I did not want to have any further contact with him. But before I was able to tell him my thoughts, he told me his, which did not differ much from mine. At least for once there had been a convergence of views.

"This is our last meeting. I will have no other session with you. You do only what you want and never follow my advice!"

Our session ended with a cold farewell from both parties. So, I was back to square one. Me and my questions!

*"The potential of one's inner course
rises from the intellectual field
of the diffuse Master-Entity
and is a course with no beginning or end."*

*From the book "The Revelation of the Entity"
by Dimitris Kakalidis.*

ACQUAINTANCE
WITH THE MASTER

The doorbell rang. Our youngest daughter, who was expecting a friend, rushed to open it. Together had come a friend of hers, whom our daughter had recently met, and had found pleasant and friendly. As I was tidying up the house, I passed in front of the open door of the room where they were sitting and chatting. Only then did I realize that we had visitors and greeted them. The young man urged me to sit with them, assuring me that they were not discussing anything personal. Wanting to take a breath, I stayed to enjoy their company.

I silently listened to their conversation. Most of the time the young man spoke, talking about some kind of Society. According to his words, they were taught to perform self-observation, something which helped them in their lives and in their relationships with other people. They also gave great importance to caring for their fellow humans and offering help. Founder of this spiritual centre, named *Omilos Eksipiretiton (the Servers' Society)*, was a Master, Dimitris Kakalidis.

I instantly wondered whether it was time to meet a Master – a meaning that I have elaborated on extensively in previous books, mainly in the series with the same title. But before barely questioning my own self, the young man addressed me, asking me if I wanted to meet their Master. My response was immediate and affirmative. He informed me that my meeting with the Master could even happen on the following day, if I was available. I arranged with the young man to go the Master's house with my car on the following afternoon. Our conversation ended and the guests along with my daughter went for a walk. I was left alone.

For the rest of the day I wondered if the man I would meet the next day was the Master I had waited for my whole life. If he could respond to my questions and if he could provide me with solutions to whatever tortured me. I had but to wait...

When we arrived at the Master's house the next day, the young man introduced us. I was startled by his appearance. He was barely forty years old. I would expect someone older, a wise old man, and certainly not someone younger than myself. What knowledge or experiences might he have that I had not acquired during the fifty years of my life? His gaze was reassuring and I thought that maybe knowledge was not associated with age after all. Besides, a look at my surroundings was solid proof that maturity of age was not an adjunct of maturity of consciousness.

After meeting the Master's wife and their two children, we all sat together and discussed a variety of topics. I told them about my life, my husband, our children, my job and they in turn informed me of the Society. Then, his wife, whose presence all this time emitted love and interest, dealt with the children, who, as were quite young, came and went throughout the house. They left the room, and so did the young man.

We were alone, the Master and I, and for some time we continued the discussion... Then the Master asked me to close my eyes to meditate. I let myself listen to his voice and what he said during the meditation. At first he instructed me to calm down and relax deeply. I began to experience within my body a current that constantly grew stronger... I interrupted the meditation and opened my eyes. I asked him what it was that I had felt, but he told me to close my eyes again and surrender myself to it. And so I did.

Then, something happened that I had never imagined. I clearly saw the organs of my body, as if looking at an x-ray. I delved, observing my heart, the veins, the invigorating blood flow, the skeleton, the muscles, all the coordinated functions of the organs. Only when the Master said that the meditation was complete did I open my eyes. I looked at him stunned. He said that now, if I can clearly see every part of my body, whenever I find something that is ill, I can directly perform self-healing. What next? A new world opened up before me that, although obvious, remained unknown to me for so many years of my life.

Until then I had believed that there was no one who could nurture such love and concern for others. The power, the current of love and the radiance that pierced me was staggering. It was an unprecedented and unbelievable experience. An experience literally indescribable. I decided that the next day I would go to the Society.

From the day of my acquaintance with the Master until today that I am writing this book, it has been thirty-three years. But the memory of our meeting lies within me, alive and intact. Even after his death in 1995, the presence of the Master still lives inside me. And there are times when I wonder... Why have not all people known a Master? The experiences beside him are a constant blessing. But every soul, every one of us, have our own choices and our own path to travel...

THE BEGINNING
OF THE DISCIPLESHIP

I was looking forward to going to the Society the next day. When I arrived I saw a lovely simple elevated two-story building. Above its wide entrance was a glass overhang that would later become the place where I would receive patients for spiritual healing or other appointments. But at the time, I did not know that I would soon decide to dedicate the rest of my life to the Society's work...

Over the years, the building itself, which continues to house the Society, has undergone many great changes. Changes made with the love and personal work of its members. But what has remained unchanged and will continue to do so, is the current of the Master's radiance permeating its space; the current that pierced me the very first time, as I crossed the Society' threshold. That was when I was convinced that the same current would overwhelm me, and I would in turn convey it to others!

The Master's disciples showed me around. All rooms had high ceilings, and were spacious, bright and clean. The furniture was scarce and old, as the financial capability of the members was limited. The Master's room was upstairs and from the large window you could see the garden's overgrown rose bush, knitting a thick layer through the courtyard between the grey apartment blocks with their dozens of windows, as prying eyes. An oasis in the centre of Athens, in every respect!

That is where we sat. In the garden's cool shade, with the playful sunrays among the green glossy leaves. The light passed filtered, similarly as through stained glass. It was the summer of 1980.

I was alone with the Master. I was left to hear his deep voice telling me to observe myself and others. Acquaintances and strangers... I cannot remember much anymore. Besides, what impressed me from our first meetings cannot be expressed in words. The only certainty was that the Master did not ask me to observe others in the way that I had learned to up to then. My preparatory work as a teacher, observing and learning from the children's reactions in order to provide them with the best possible care, was contributory. But now my observation was called to be more incisive and substantial. Because its purpose was that over time, I would learn to recognize in others their true nature – which in itself was the initial basic assistance I could offer them!

Most of the disciples who were close to the Master had already come a year before I met him. I was wondering about the fact that I was fifty years old, while the other disciples were much younger than me. Should I think of myself as something of a mother to them? At one time, I was proud of the age difference between myself and my cousins, of the fact that I was the oldest and therefore the most rational. Here, however, this was not the case. If I hurried and progressed rapidly in my discipleship would I catch up to them? But the Master reminded us that rushing puts many obstacles and causes us to trip ourselves up, ultimately not helping at all. Certainly, however, consciousness achievements were not a function of the longer duration of the teaching someone received. And they were not proportional to age, either, judging by my own self.

Some more time passed before I realized the importance of such a difference in ages. This difference of mine would provide me with the opportunity to describe numerous experiences, positive or negative, that I had acquired before even meeting the Master, and which would be useful to the younger students. Life experiences that I was called to redeem!

One day, the Master and his wife came to my home. My husband was away on a business trip abroad so he did not have the opportunity to meet them, something that would happen later anyhow. I had asked them to take a look at the room in which I would work and meditate in order to tell me if there was anything better I could do. They did not notice anything that might prevent or hamper my work so we sat in the living room where we discussed various matters. I suggested cooking something quick so that we could all have lunch together and they accepted.

I went to the kitchen and when the food was ready, we sat at the table, where I served them. We continued to talk in general, about the discipleship as well as about certain issues of my own. When we finished the meal, they thanked me and bid me farewell, telling me that we would meet again in a few hours, in the afternoon, at the Society.

A while passed since then. I was informed that the Master's wife and children would be away for the day, so I decided to prepare a meal and take it to him before lunchtime. When the Master tasted it, he told me with a smile that it was not very good and politely placed it aside. I was at a loss for words, and asked him why he had not told me something similar the other day, when they had come to my house. He explained to me that I had only just started my discipleship and I would not have accepted such a remark. It is possible that I would have been offended, deciding to discontinue my discipleship, since I had not yet accepted and trusted the Master.

Given a chance, he explained that for the same reason he had also refrained from telling me about the room which I had prepared for my meditation. I listened carefully as he analysed to me how my room was too busy with ornaments and trinkets, many of them old or emotionally charged, which ultimately, instead of beautifying, only gave weight. Half-jokingly, and in order for me to better understand, he described an image of the ornaments on the shelves grumbling, screaming, quarrelling or complaining. Until then, I had never thought of it that way.

Meanwhile, I remembered the words of my husband and later of one of our daughters, telling me that my cooking was not very good. I mentioned it to the Master, without of course believing he could give me a magic formula that would make me a chef. But, unexpectedly, the Master did have such a recipe for me.

"When you cook, do it with love."

It might not always have the best flavour, but my cooking has since improved substantially in terms of quality: the meals are indeed lighter. The secret ingredient was love, as it was for anything else I did, although it took considerable effort and years of discipleship to learn how to remain stable in this position.

As my discipleship progressed, I increasingly found that I was ignorant of various words used by the Master and his disciples. I knew their interpretation in daily life but I ignored the particular connotation attributed by the Master; words such as *synthesis, diffusion, field, alignment, entity,* as well as several others. I searched through dictionaries for their meanings, their real sense, I wrote them down in a notebook and cross-checked them with the explanations the Master provided me.

The Master said that the era we live in is that of *synthesis.* As humanity conquers a consciousness field, it proceeds to the next, which it is now called upon to realize. But, this is not easily accomplished. People insist to express previous fields, either individually or collectively. They mistakenly believe that they give them certainty and assurance. Therefore, the disciples are those who are called to lead the way and be the first to realize the new fields. Thus, in the era of synthesis, one of many things the disciples do is to accept the dual, as they erroneously consider, substance of themselves, of things and situations, in other words the positive and the negative; to equilibrate and experience their union, which automatically leads to a higher range. Then, they transfer the life current, which is none other than the synthesis of all facets.

"What are disciples for, if the task is always performed by the Masters?" It was reasonable to ask.

"Because both are needed to realize the task," he replied. "The Master has the knowledge, which he conveys to the disciples, to the extent that they are ready. The disciples begin to imitate the Master at any level they are capable of and, in turn, through their way of life, they show other people how they too can improve their own lives."

I had nothing more to ask. I simply felt significant gratitude that I had the good fortune of meeting the Master and being his disciple in *the teaching of synthesis* he provided us. My task was the stability in the position of discipleship and confidence in the spiritual field. And I was determined to realize this.

GREAT WOMAN
OR DISCIPLE?

Gradually, I began showing the Master my paintings. He looked at them carefully, each time analysing what I was ready to accept. I had begun painting again, but as time passed, I painted less and less. Furthermore, during that period, I had set about writing texts in the manner of courses for members of the Society. The Master encouraged this decision of mine, although memories came to mind from when I was back at school. Inhibitory circumstances, which had left a negative impact on my writing. Only when studying in the United States, had I begun to realize my innate inclination for writing. And the Master who knew all of my unexpressed potential, urged me, preparing me to write books; books on my experience next to him and the teaching he gave us.

My writings, over time, improved. Only then, and as I was ready for it, did the Master explain to me that I was not a painter. That was not the task I was meant to do. My father had told me the same thing, but now had come the fullness of time, the result of my discipleship, and I was ready to accept it. Moreover, I realized that everything the Master told me contained not the slightest inkling of rejection, unlike what I received from others, whenever they told me something similar. And this was the main difference! So I oriented towards writing and focused on it.

Over time, I wrote several texts about my discipleship and the teaching. I read them to the Master and he provided various outlooks on the correctness or not of what I had understood and documented. The time came when he told me that I was ready to write books. In fact, he suggested the theme of the first one should be the woman and her role within society, her essential position as a woman. I started immediately...

Whenever I completed a chapter, I read it to him so that he could validate or correct what I had written or even, if I must, throw it out. Such work was not easy. Based on the teaching, I had to mention and analyse important issues in easily understood writing that would, at the same time, leave no room for misinterpretations.

When the first book was completed, the next one came on the role of man, and following that was the one on the role of the couple. They were published on my fourth and fifth year of my discipleship respectively, and I always continued reading what I had written to the Master, as I in fact did for each of my following books.

Next book? On spiritual healing. This was the proposal of the Master and, admittedly, I wanted it too. I had the title certainly ready, but the bulk of the work remained. And this time it was harder than previous books.

With respect to the treatment of diseases by classical medicine, I had to highlight the spiritual work as our Master taught us, as well as how the disciples, including myself, worked. The matters I dealt with needed considerable discussion with the Master, who, in addition, gave me various meditations for further elaboration. In the seventh year of my discipleship, the book was published. Soon, there were some who showed interest and came to the Society seeking healings or a discipleship on how to become healers.

But a little later, something unexpected happened. So many people began coming that we literally did not have time to talk to them all! Most had been informed of our action from a newspaper of wide circulation. One of its columnists was a nutritionist, a research associate of the Centre for Alternative Medicine, who had for several days been mentioning the book of Spiritual Healing.

There were several who contacted us by mail or phone, as they lived outside Athens. They explained their problem and requested a healing. To meet this demand, we began operating the mail section. Our members who lived outside Athens could now receive the necessary courses for training as healers.

Thus, a new need arose; that of written courses-texts on the teaching and the necessary knowledge for a spiritual healer. Curiously, just as I started writing them, a number of problems made their appearance, seeking my interest and my time to solve them. One disciple was transferred to the KAT hospital with a broken leg, while the parents of another disciple, without providing any explanations, asked her to leave their family home. Not to mention of course the financial difficulties faced by many of the disciples. The result of all this was a strong headache, which of course prevented me from writing.

I had but to discuss it with the Master, who indeed simplified matters within me. He explained that it was natural for various difficulties and impediments to arise. Against the position I now finally expressed, in other words to work as a healer and convey to others the concept of the spiritual field, these resistances were expected. The fact that I did not understand or had not evaluated the affairs in that way, did not mean they ceased to exist. Humanity's resistances existed, whether they were unconsciously expressed or not, and functioned in an inhibitory fashion, complicating the disciples in their development. The Master's analysis was quite reassuring. In fact, as soon as he stopped talking, we were informed of the registration of a new member who had come for the first time to the Society. My headache immediately disappeared.

The next day, I started writing the first course on the training of spiritual healers. When I read it to the Master that afternoon, he told me that I had not yet expressed stability for the projection and spreading of spiritual healing or the Society's books. He explained that this was due to the resistance and fear to externalize the disciple. The words of the Master gave an answer to similar thoughts that had already been troubling me and which I wanted to overcome.

After many meditations, insights and quests, I wrote the second lesson. The Master approved it and even told me that he considered it to be of an academic level. It was some time until I decided to write the third lesson. The Master continued giving us new elements of the teaching, while helping us assimilate previous ones.

When I read him the third lesson, he found it good but not inspired. As he told me, it was not a text written by a disciple who had been receiving teachings for seven years, but from a lady who remains in her human functions. I had already noticed the lack of flow in the text as I read it, something which I had not realized when I was writing it. I agreed with him and I accepted to write it again, while the Master told me that he would wait for the result.

It was several days of analyses, regimens, meditations... Finally, without a doubt, I realized what was preventing me from completing the third lesson. The problem was my selfish desire to write with skills and knowledge that I considered my own, and not through my union with the Entity. The Master was absolutely right. I had written a text as a lady with the capacity of an author, appropriating the knowledge and talent, and not as a disciple working in the flow. I had fallen into the trap of wanting to be and look great! But eventually, unwittingly renouncing the disciple that I was, all I had accomplished was the exact opposite. Having confined myself to my own abilities and possibilities, I was trapped in the knowledge of my personality. And my personality did not know anything, except for wanting to seem great. Projecting myself, I had, on my own, blocked the view to the vast plains of knowledge, and from my writing quiver I had displaced the Entity, which granted me the gift to perform each task. I confined myself to my small human potential, and therefore to my weaknesses, thus ceasing to be that empty container, ready to accept to become a conductor of the uninterrupted flow of knowledge and solutions. I resigned of my desire to write!

The third lesson was written, we might say, of itself. I was just a hand that grounded the knowledge to the alphabet, the true wisdom teachings of spiritual reality. The word *"nenikikamen"* – *"we have won"* – sounded through me, and the experience of personality coordination with spiritual expression was liberating. Since then, I engaged even more vigorously in the dissemination of spiritual healing and the teaching through the books I had already written.

The need for the expansion of each of us and the spreading of the teaching is necessary. The externalization of the spiritual field is inherent in everyone and everything, it is realized primarily with the awareness of its existence. And all this would be done with simplicity.

LIFE EXAMPLE

My need for sleep had begun to decline significantly, as did its duration. The unexplained tiredness I had felt for the past years before coming to the Society had now been... sufficiently explained. My refusal to deal with everyday situations that had become a torturous routine without meaning, the avoidance of my own thoughts, of my relationships with others, and ultimately of life itself, had implemented unconsciously, or even consciously, a defensive withdrawal mechanism. Difficulties plunged me to a loss, a daydream and an *astral state* which, as expected, brought with them sleepiness and fatigue. I fell into apathy and indifference, refusing to move into action for anything, and this situation merely worsened the sleepiness and the fatigue. Now however, despite my fewer hours of sleep, I would wake up without fatigue. I had found the Master and hence essence in life!

Many times I had seen dreams worthy of note that had something to teach me. On the path of discipleship, even dreams could be used as a tool for further insights and revelations.

In one of them, I saw the Master sitting in an armchair with closed eyes, reaching out his hand to grab a glass. He groped for it, but there was no glass.

"Master, there is no glass. Do not search in vain," I said to him.

"Really, Mrs Klairi?" He wondered. "If there was, I would grab it and drink from it. I would quench my thirst even if the glass was empty!"

"Seriously, Master?" I asked surprised.

"Of course, Mrs Klairi, and this shows how important an idea in our mind is," he replied and stopped concerning himself with the glass or the water, as if he was no longer thirsty.

That is what I saw in my dream, and when I woke up I realized that there are indeed things that exist beyond human logic. How many things was I ignorant of! What immediately came to mind was that the Master's knowledge was not something he *had*; it was something he *was*. And the light of this knowledge is self-existent within us, but has not yet been realized. Each of us is trained to discover it and to bathe in its radiance.

I was thirsty for an understanding of the new world that had opened up before me and within me, this essential dimension of things behind logicisms through which we have learned to function and understand everything around us. And the teaching quenched my thirst.

Steadily following the discipleship, I achieved the continuous expansion of my perspective and of my being; a path that resulted in freedom. And the more liberated I was of my small thoughts, the more I desired to convey the teaching to my fellow humans so that they too could in turn be helped. And the more I cared about them, the more liberated I became, and ready to accept even more, deeper elements of what the Master uninterruptedly taught us.

From the very first year of my discipleship, I realized that the Master-disciple relationship is a relationship of attraction between two consciousness fields. The Master is a consciousness field much wider than the human one, but, at the same time, he turns towards humans in order to help and educate them. How many times had I wondered when we too will acquire his conscious experience and simultaneously his experienced consciousness...

All that the Master taught us he possessed absolutely, without any doubts or transitions. In union with everything, he conveyed to each one of us the elements necessary to express what we were searching for, great or small, whether we were aware of it or denied it in our ignorance. The Master, without impatience, waited for us to mature and to manifest the respective levels of consciousness.

His function was a constant surprise to us all. His actions and words flowed from a dimension that we still ignored. So whenever I conquered a field, the Master would come to augment and enrich it. The purpose of the new impetus was further expansion and so the Master constantly caused vibrations in my consciousness in order for me to increasingly learn to care about others.

As my discipleship continued, the Master's stimuli were accepted with greater ease and faith, because, at the same time, my confidence in him, through the proven examples of my life, grew even more. This confidence, which had now been built and strengthened within me, was redemptive. Merely the acceptance of the Master brought the required flow in our lives and opened up redeeming paths for us all.

I had just completed a meditation, but my question remained unanswered. Nevertheless, the texture of my questions differentiated in relation to before. Back then, I questioned the essence of life and the meaning of our own existence, while now, I knew that they existed and took action to experience them all the more. The books, the almost inexhaustible knowledge that existed within them, had rendered us theoretical scientists of life. I was no longer an ignorant little girl whose uncle's knowledge impressed her. I previously sought knowledge to cover the voids within, but the only thing I gained was empty theories, study without practice. I wondered then if there is some kind of task carried out in the world; I now knew that there in fact was, and wondered what my involvement in it was and how to act on it.

Going outside, I found the Master seated in the Society's garden, his presence permeating the area. Just by looking at him, I realized that he was redeemed. It was clear to me that the redemption of our *ego* leads us to an ever greater expression of spirituality. And judging by the Master's example, this required love towards everyone, union with their needs, their pains and their fears.

Deep understanding of things and union with them also brought about greater awareness. Besides, understanding is part of expressing this awareness. And, really, is there anything more important than the knowledge that spirit and matter, including our bodies, are one and the same? Our Master made the analysis that whoever reaches this level of consciousness passes to enlightenment.

Enlightenment was a word that I also heard often, when I first started going to the Society. I partly knew its meaning and so did not ask for an explanation. I expected to acquire a broader understanding of its meaning through the teaching in general. But while understanding of its meaning was in my hand, enlightenment itself was not; it is a decision of the Entity.

I often wondered what an entity does, where it is, what it expects, or if it even expects anything at all. I wondered if it meditated or not. It was reasonable to ask whether it was beyond meditation, being united with everything. I wondered, but naturally, I saw no answers coming. Was this perhaps also a lesson I had a hard time accepting? Eventually, I accepted that my questions would remain unanswered and relaxed knowing that the entities are further away from us.

I was called to follow the example of the Master, requesting firmly and irrevocably for the Entity's supervision. My admiration for his teaching grew day by day, with each new analysis he made. And then, my example, or another disciple's example, would strengthen the position of the rest, who might still be wavering, until it established itself and become stable. In this way, the work of the teaching continues to spread from one to the other.

UNDERTAKING RESPONSIBILITY

I often forgot to invoke the supervision of the spiritual field. The result of this unconscious function of mine was a feeling of constriction in fear of making mistakes whenever I undertook any task. I could not stand any imperfection and weakness of my character, and especially could not bear the thought of others seeing them.

The same thing happened when the Master suggested I give lectures in Athens and in other cities in order to spread the teaching. The embarrassment I felt then, simply at the thought of what I had to do, brought about an intense redness to my face. As this continued, the Master, to make things easy on me, proposed that the lecture be given at the Society's premises, where I would analyse its work.

Some time later, a disciple started talking about the spreading of the work. Without any previous knowledge, she brought forth the issue of the lectures, even proposing that I undertake them. Her union with the Master, even if she was unaware of it, was a further mobilization for their realization. I began meditating on this matter, until I realized that it was just a simple task, and eventually began it without shyness or blushing.

The days passed and the Master, recognizing that something was troubling me, summoned me and asked me what the issue concerning me was. I replied that it was irrelevant with the lectures; it was my insecurity of whether the disciples rejected all I that did. I was referring to my discussions with the new members, including from how I dressed to what time I arrived at the Society. Even the minimal chance of them expressing such an attitude discouraged me from taking on any responsibility for the work, even though I knew that in doing so the discipleship I was receiving would not be manifested.

That was when the Master told me about the flow – the flow within me that would be expressed only if I allowed it to exist, something which I did not do for various reasons. I replied that I was aware of the existence of this internal flow, but did not understand what it was that prevented its expression, adding that it may occur after years, who knew? The Master insisted that if the flow exists, it would not delay.

After all that we had discussed, I followed a course that at times led me to a chaotic situation, while at other times brought a revival within me that was expressed with the flow. And when difficulties intervened, I resumed focusing on it, to be reborn again.

One of the disciples made a proposal to me with which the Master agreed. He asked me to take on a self-study group, his own, as he saw its members gradually leave it because they did not feel that they could respond to what he was telling them. Of course, as in all groups, what is conveyed is the teaching, but, in this case, these members might have had to be dealt with in a different manner. Although their need for a discipleship was great because of the many difficulties they encountered, they still progressed very slowly.

I did not answer him immediately, as I wanted to think about it. It was the first time I would undertake such a group, and most certainly preferred members with more fervour. But the need for improving their lives was calling for me to provide them with whatever aid I could offer. Besides, a service, whatever it may be, is always expressed by the position of offering, without expectation for the particular result which I might have desired for them. The Master was always exceptionally clear when he told us to selflessly offer to all! And this selflessness, with the purity meant by the Master, did not have room for the expectation or anticipation of others to even follow the discipleship.

At the incident with my acquaintance, many years ago, when I had advised her on how to handle her relationship, I clearly sought no profit of my own. But I sought the validation of my words, I wanted her to agree to implement them and to bring about a result. But, even if I had assumed that what I told her was right, still, I should not have expected that of her.

I eventually accepted the proposal and proceeded to meet with the members the next day and inform them that I would take on their group. I had now decided to not be indifferent towards anyone, but to pass into action without fear and without attachments and resistances.

One of those days, I was approached by a girl, a younger member, who told me that a gentleman had come for the first time to our premises. He was interested in talking to someone who could inform him on the work we did, its aim, and if he too could participate. But he had said nothing to her of himself, and neither about his profession, nor his age; he had not even mentioned his name. I replied that I would meet this gentleman myself, after discussing it with the Master. I went immediately to his room and repeated what the girl had told me.

For decades my behaviour had been dictated by the social norms I had grown up with. And these, among oth-

ers, stated that we must be formally polite and, therefore, always introduce ourselves. I was brought up with
the, by default false, respectability of the bourgeois, and I
was accustomed to talking in the polite plural even to my
mother, and so manners consistent with good upbring-
ing, but lacking in courtesy of the soul, would spring up
every now and then during the early years of my discipleship.

His response was instantaneous and silencing. "Have
you ever heard the Master caring about the profession,
the beliefs or anything else about a person, even what
one's name is? What always concerns me is only the person that is within and what path he or she wishes to follow in order to evolve. Ignore what has been conveyed to
you and immediately go to see him. Focus on him, giving
him what he is ready to receive."

Leaving his room, I once again consolidated something
I realized from my very first meeting with him, when I
had visited him at his home. He had been interested in
everything related to me because he was interested in
me, and for no other reason.

I finally discussed with the gentleman, who willing-
ly and without question told me his name. Perhaps the
interest I showed in him was the reason for which he
opened up. Our conversation covered topics troubling
him, and how the discipleship might help him deal with
them. As he was leaving, he asked to meet again in two

days, something which continued for a short while, until he finally decided to become a member.

The moment came when the Master asked me if I wanted to be president of the Society. For a while I left the question hovering unanswered. The delay of my decision was due to the events back at the *American College*, when the teachers had felt that I was unworthy to be president of the classes. Since then, whenever anyone would propose something similar to me, I would immediately decline. But the Master was not anyone. He always referred to the spiritual field, as we, his disciples, also learned to do.

How life turns out sometimes! Eventually, after mature reflection, I made my decision, which was positive, and have continued to be president of the Society since then.

Apart from the literary work and the spiritual healing, I had also undertaken various other matters concerning the Society. In addition to the lectures, I investigated the possibility of distributing the books of *Megas Seirios Publications* – that were under the Society's aegis – in Greece and abroad, while I also inspected other buildings to see if they were appropriate for extending our premises, while at the same time dealing with many other issues.

From the beginning of our discipleship, each of us was responsible for various matters, such as self-study groups, hospital visits, personal appointments with members and more. But as my age progressed, I began focusing on literary work and spiritual healing, which is what the Master had begun teaching me from our very first meeting.

Despite being devoted to the Society's work, we also participated in all other events of daily life; in our work, in the care of our homes, in visits to relatives and friends, as well as in the joys of other disciples, whether it concerned a wedding, a success, or anything else. But, as is only natural, we all went through various events in our lives, sometimes pleasant and sometimes unpleasant. So, if someone had to take care of a member of their family who was ill, they would necessarily attend the Society's work with frequent interruptions. Then, and for as long as was needed, they would hand over the work under their responsibility to another disciple.

This happened to me when my father fell ill and had to stay for two months in the hospital. I remember that both he and my husband, when I first started going to the Society and after explaining to them the work I did there, told me to make every effort, stressing their support in my decision to take on a discipleship. Just one day after my father returned home, my mother suffered a strained arm, so we once again had to return to the hospital. For as long as their care lasted, I would visit them two to three times a day. Fortunately, their home was close to ours. Our eldest daughter, whenever she had time from work, would also facilitate me by spending a few hours taking care of them, so that I could immediately leave for the Society.

An essential lesson was and is the selfless offer to all. And the only offer the Master accepted from others was their participation in the Society's work with each one's capability. From a repair to the premises and a donation for the publication of a new book, to taking on the responsibility of a group and the dissemination of the teaching.

The teaching of synthesis was evident from the first step I took in the Society and with what I saw being done in it. In addition to the work in the inner field, a number of practical tasks was also being carried out, such as, for example, painting the walls a different colour. These were flows that were brought about and directed by the Master. The education of the disciples was performed in all manners and it was often difficult at first for someone to understand the importance of some of them. But, in reality, there were no external and internal functions, as all functions were internal!

REDEMPTION OF THE PAST

Although reduced, the various difficulties within me continued to exist. One of them reappeared when the Master asked me to take on the Society's financial matters. From the beginning of my discipleship I had pointed out to him that the cause of my fear of any kind of duty assignment regarding financial matters was the effect of my mother's words when I was still a child. This fear accompanied me throughout the course of my entire life and I continued propagating it to my husband, our children, relatives and acquaintances, even when concerning a financial matter that had been concluded.

But for the Master, what was obviously desired was to overcome this repulsion of mine. He told me to stop dealing with the past anymore; there is only the present that contributes to the development of the future. It was quite some time until I was persuaded to take on the Society's financial matters, and I soon realized that my fear had been increasingly diminishing.

I sought ways to improve the Society's finances, but in vain. I could not find anything that could help the situation, apart from trivial recipes that only brought meagre and hasty results. I racked my brain for specific solutions until I realized that I need not be looking for fundraising methods. These had already been provided by the Master. The only thing needed of me was their realization.

But what were the methods, or more correctly the main method, that the Master had provided? It was none other, of course, than the grounding of a concept, of an idea almost inconceivable, which, if someone has not substantially touched it, might consider it as a theory touching upon the limits of science fiction; another abstract bombast arousing the fanciful minds of the devotees of mysticism and alchemy. Because that is where so many unrealized spiritual truths end up. And this truth is none other than the fact that matter and spirit are one and the same!

For centuries and under historical circumstances which are not of this time to analyse, spiritual people distanced themselves and their work from matter and repelled material abundance. The result was that matter, including money, came to be owned mostly by cunning individuals and its manipulation by them was exclusively self-centred. Nowadays, however, a repolarization of matter is required, a reinstatement to its true basis and its link to the spiritual field that will put it to use for the task of offering towards the fellow human. This, in fact, would also be its redemption!

One disciple mentioned that they would like to hear about the experiences I had gained due to my age, which of course they did not have. So I recounted various events and the following day I also brought them some pictures. Among them were my teachers' letters from the university in the United States, given to me as references, in which they noted my pleasant character. Also among them were various letters from my fellow students, who wrote flattering remarks about my body. However, an issue that I had described in detail to the Master was my difficulty in accepting the thickness of my legs below my ankles; something which that day I decided to share with that group of disciples. The Master suggested I get up and walk through the room, which initially caused me slight discomfort, although I knew that whatever he did was in order to expand our consciousness. Only then did I realize that certain disciples had thus far not noticed the thickness of my legs, this terrible problem for me, which

I had been trying to hide throughout my adolescence. The Master told me that their thickness showed a firm stance, in other words an inclination to be grounded. Suddenly, from the lifetime negative colours with which I had painted a particular feature of mine, its true nature appeared a redemptive truth that I alone could have never managed to de-symbolize.

The Master's analyses of physical characteristics, such as weight, height, or even the size of the feet, were revealing, but not dogmatically applicable to every case. For example, he told us that wide feet usually show a range of ideas, while very small ones often meant their owners had ideas that absorbed them, being stuck to them persistently. Our body is projected with shortcomings through which we are educated, but despite the many features that we perceive as defects, each body is nevertheless an expression of the spiritual field.

We are often entrenched in the idea we have of ourselves; a restrictive idea that we acquire from our entrapment in the form. The focus on the body, our own or others', without realizing the spiritual current and the true nature, our own and our body's, as taught by the Master, makes us small, weak, and isolated living beings. Several times, indeed, he analysed how we seek vibrations in our body from intense and heavy shocks, advising us to move on to more subtle vibrations. I noticed that I had been experiencing both – the heaviness, usually of desires, as well as the refinement.

"Desire is also love, and this is achieved only if love is not coloured as a desire," the Master said.

I had understood the difference between love and desire, but I was not aware that both are the same, since we consider them different and opposite. I worked systematically in order not to colour love. In my meditations I saw myself dissipating the energy to all parts of my body, which, due to ignorance and resistances, prevented spiritual expression. I mentioned my meditations to the Master and he told me to remain in this position.

For some time, I continued showing the Master what I painted. And it was a surprise to me when he sometimes requested paper and pencil to also paint. Many of these paintings did not reflect the reality how I logically perceived it, and within me I characterized them as fantastic and bizarre. I could not grasp their symbolism, but I would not discuss it with the Master. I waited to figure it out on my own...

One day after finishing painting, we put on our coats and, as we were coming down the stairs to leave, the Master asked one of the disciples if he liked surrealism.

"Certainly," he replied, adding that it was an art movement that greatly pleased him. The same question was also asked of me. And, as expected, I answered that I did not understand what was portrayed in surrealism...

"Therefore, I do not like it at all," I replied.

"I did not expect to hear that from you, Mrs Klairi!" He said, supposedly startled. "In all your travels, you must certainly have seen surrealistic paintings in the museums you have obviously visited. How can you say you do not like this high expression of art?"

I did not know what to answer. I only said that I would think about it and have another look at the relevant paintings. But, this particular issue was not the only retrospect I would be making towards my past...

As time passed, I asked him about various issues concerning my past. Among them, I told him of my accidental meeting with our family acquaintance who had informed me of the association from which I eventually got the scholarship, as well as the meeting with the dance teacher and all he had told me. The Master confirmed his words, on the joy and freedom offered by those actions stemming from our true nature, but disagreed with me in the notion of randomness that I had mentioned. He told me that nothing is random. Everything, unforeseen or not, that happens to us and that we call coincidence or random events and which seem to determine the favourable or unfavourable outcome of our lives, are events that we ourselves have caused and attracted. They are circumstances that are projected in response to our need and to our request to move forward and evolve.

To this analysis I should also integrate the event in Amerikis Square that had scarred me as a child. Although cruel, it wanted to teach me something while simultaneously asking something of me. What is certain is that it shows the immaturity of humanity that literally bled through its prolonged adolescent outbreak, urging it to brutally childish manifestations, to assertion, competition and violence.

It was inevitable, therefore, to mention to the Master my decades-long thought on the established limits of age periods that do not necessarily correspond to their actual realization.

"Mankind has not yet reached adulthood but is still in its adolescence," I heard the Master say, "as you have perceived. It is a necessary step, since in this period many different aspects are expressed that must be harmonized in order for humans to move to the next level. You may wonder why adulthood has not yet been displayed, as humankind appeared on the planet thousands of years ago. It is not surprising if we remember that it passed through several stages, learning to walk, eating appropriately, or pronouncing words and turning them into sentences. And thus, it reached adolescence which is an essential period, as it prepares for adulthood that very few substantially express."

So, this search of mine for my substantial coming of age was what had urged me to the futile appeal for help from the psychiatrist. I did not forget to mention that adventure too, as well as its inglorious ending. But this time, the Master did not need to tell me anything. All those events in my life belong to the past. And along with them, the futility that from time to time oppressed my life, the feeling of unfulfillment, the concern for my children, my excruciatingly unanswered questions, my disappointments and the anxiety to be *somebody*, had been burned out through my discipleship; my regeneration process besides the Master, with the teaching as a tool.

Even the apathy, the indifference I had always projected in order to avoid coming into conflict with the views of others, such as for example with my husband's, and later with my son's, when they persistently obsessed for hours with meaningless issues, was a matter for discussion with the Master if it continued to manifest itself. And with his help, I worked to overcome it as soon as possible.

"There is neither right nor wrong," he said. How right he was! "Both are expressed by humanity and are fields projected by it. What I always tell disciples is to seek what is fair through the position of the disciple."

I knew now that nothing was able to stand in the way of my ever increasing inner expansion, none of those shackles that, if we think about it, we impose on ourselves, could stop my progress or hold me back. The barriers that once rendered me uninvolved in life turned into springboards for deepening and transformed to initiatory processes!

ASPECTS OF THE UNIVERSE

I had already been going through the third year of my discipleship and although my faith, both in the teaching and in the union with our true nature, would be proven to me, the identification with certain aspects of my own and of others had not stopped.

I often mentioned to the Master the difficulties I had with my husband, my children, with those who I generally came into contact and our relationships caused friction. At first, his reply troubled me. He told me that everything in the world are aspects of our own! By accepting these aspects, all of the aspects projected by our fellow humans that we probably do not like, we help them to accept these aspects themselves and to then gradually change.

It was not uncommon for me to resist accepting certain of the elements he taught us. Indeed, I sometimes even got angry at him. I found it inconceivable to accept that, for example, even the aspect of the murderer, the criminal, the paranoid, were our own and that they asked of us to redeem them. I could by no means accept that within me existed the inhuman function of the black marketeers I had seen hanging in Amerikis Square, along with the disgraceful violence of their executioners. They and I were two very different things. And so this intense reaction of mine continued throughout the first year of my discipleship.

But no matter how difficult and strange it may sound, I gradually managed to understand and to accept it. In essence, the effective example of the Master himself, who accepted everyone unconditionally, contributed to this. Never in my entire life have I witnessed such a function in anyone else. Yes, though unexpressed, I had inside me all aspects of the world, positive and negative, and I was called to uplift them, seeing in them what we call the 'agatho'* no matter the difficulties.

We concern ourselves with all others! This has become my alpha and omega. A first stage of implementation,

---

*The term "agatho" out of the Greek word 'αγαθό' is used to mean all that is beyond the duality of good and bad. It is the Entity, the Whole, the Monad.

common to us all, of the care we learn to show to others, is in the relationships within our families. The same happened to me before starting my discipleship. I loved my husband, but even in this relationship, I was not always giving. And despite the will I manifested, I often had setbacks. But if I had by then realized that he is an aspect of mine, would that have altered my attitude towards him? And, would it have helped him change? I did not know the answer and so waited to hear the Master's.

But since I had now realized what I had to do, why did I not implement it? I remembered then that the Master had told us that even if we have not fully expressed the stance, we deliver it to the Entity and we simply continue implementing it without dealing with our shortcomings and difficulties.

His analysis gave me something new that perhaps I had been avoiding until then, possibly because I did not want to see my own negative aspects. And yet, it was I that had spoken with impertinence to our relative, back then, and again I and my bad character that had pushed away my friend when his words became a mirror for me to clearly see my reflection. But I was not only that; because it was I again who realized my mistake and lowered my head asking for forgiveness. The acceptance of myself was the most difficult because the aspects stemmed from my own self. Then I thought that I had not at all realized our true nature.

There were times when I repeated the immature events of the past, something that did not help me at all. The Master told me not to pay attention to them, but to meditate on the essence. This I did and a current of love and union with everyone passed through me. His presence, his help, is always within me and I experience it as soon as I turn to the broadness of the spiritual field. There is no longer my need to be great, nor my fear that I am incompetent. Even when these contradictions become instantaneous experiences, I immediately dissolve them by consistently following the entity of the Master that leads me to the one Self.

Our ignorance, needless repetitions and desires exist simply because we seek to meet a Master, even if we are not able to realize it. We seek to follow a teaching that will lead us to the recognition of our true nature. Then our life will not be a continuous torment, but shall become a miracle which begets happiness and bliss.

One morning I woke up feeling great displeasure. I had been working on one of my books and I realized I had made a significant error. I did not wonder why errors are made, since the Master had previously given his analysis on the subject. Errors bring a stimulus to the disciples, urging them to investigate their causes and overcome them. But empirically I also knew something else: an error leads to fear that, if not delivered to the Entity, continues to exist and to expand.

I remembered something from when my children were still young, or when I worked at the kindergarten. When a baby cries, it unconsciously pins its fear or any other condition, on its mother, who, with her care, exempts it of its difficulty. So, if I too was delivering my mistake to the Entity, not only would it show me how to correct it, letting me pass on to fearlessness, but it would also solve it for me.

Although I understood what the Master taught us, I continued to fear for my errors, also feeling various pains in the areas of my head, back, and legs. It was clear that the delivery of my error was not total. I wondered how it would be complete and realized that love was my only tool. Love slowly overwhelmed me and I began to be discharged of my problems. Its current flooded me and dissolved the mistakes, pains and fears that previously existed. I felt very well, experiencing love and passing it on to everyone and everything. What was left for me to do? Just one more thing – to have stability in the love that dissolves what is projected from our own selves; the fears, the pains, the mistakes.

The Master said that the universe exists within us; within every human, and that each of us is everything. He had repeatedly told us and I had by then begun to understand and to mentally conceive it, but it was not becoming an experience.

I was alone at home, and so I started reciting one of
the Master's hymns. Something inside me started to dif-
ferentiate, even in my senses. I remained for some time
steady in this minimal change with the faith that stability would bring about the desired result. And then the
experience would become true knowledge.

Gradually, I began to conceive that something vast
passed through me. As I continued, it became more and
more profound. My self expanded and simultaneously
spread and included the world, the whole universe. The
Master's words, that the mind and the heart are necessary to intersect, sounded within me. Thus, knowledge
of the mind descends into the heart and the love of the
heart rises to the mind. When this was achieved I started to experience a completely different feel. I was actually the universe. And every human and all that existed
around us were the universe.

I stayed for hours in this state, internally thanking
the Master for the path he gave me. And then I thought
about the teaching of synthesis again. That which unifies
a tiny part of the whole, like ourselves, with the entire
vast universe. This cannot be conceived by our senses
nor with descriptions, but only when experienced. Then
I realized my breadth. For its full realization to come to
each of us, the prior decision to work for others is necessary.

"The engagement of the disciples with identifications," the Master analysed, "distract them from the realization of any specific task they are called to do. They waste their time and suffer various charges after retaining the energy and not utilizing it on a specific task to expand the tasks they have undertaken.

The negative elements expressed by the disciples are aspects that come to light for all to see and learn. The Master provides a teaching, inviting his disciples to go beyond them and to redeem them. Their reactions, such as fear of rejection, jealousy for others, and many more, are due to an incorrect assumption that they themselves are not in the Spirit, the essence of their nature. This has nothing to do with the truth, because we are all there, as long as we recognize it."

One day, I mentioned to the Master that I was feeling an indefinable discomfort. He, with unexpected simplicity, told me that it was the expected result for all the unpleasantries we observe in ourselves. We are in a hurry to succeed while at the same time projecting fear that what we ask for will not be achieved. We are upset at the thought that we will never manage to accept the repulsive aspects of ourselves and we will not stop denying them. Haste is an aspect of the personality. Only if we accept the personality will it in turn accept its own aspects, such as haste. He asked me to calm down and to meditate.

As I immersed in meditation, the fear left, leaving clarity in its place. My thoughts became clear, and so did my intuition. The love for my own self grew... Only then was I able to see and understand that haste and fear had become the tool to reveal that I was looking for something much broader, that I wanted to realize something much more important. The haste, the fear, all the aspects of our personality, the personality itself, educates and is educated. That was an important step in its acceptance, simply as an aspect of myself. Through the love that I had experienced for myself, I embraced and accepted it. A sensation of brightness spread throughout me and around me, and for the first time I was free. So, this was the freedom which the Master spoke of! I so much wanted its stability not to be subject to the known vacillations.

I told him of all the realizations I had made during my meditation. He told me that meditation is necessary to be repeated in order for the experience of freedom to become embedded in me. And, of course, as the matter in question was in any case freedom, there was absolutely no restriction in necessarily following this particular meditation. What was important was the constant repetition that leads to the consolidation and not the entrapment in a convenient and proven regime.

We all need to understand the true nature, the stable and irreversible, from which are projected the phenomena whose forms constantly vary. Only then will we realize that the positive and negative elements come to us to prove who our real self is and how it can be set free!

REACTIONS

My discipleship progressed... In the past, I would re-act strongly to the reprimands of others, even if they were justified, as had happened with the acquaintance who had pointed out my bad behaviour. The same also hap-pened later when my husband tried to make me under-stand all of the car's mechanical parts, as was the case with my disagreement with the psychiatrist. But with the Master, it was different. Recognizing in him the love he showed towards everyone and the support he offered in our own development, I was much more receptive to any of his reprimands.

However, this did not happen always. Often my per-sonality kicked in, as we say, clouding my perception and preventing me from seeing and experiencing his love. In fact, I reacted so much that I began doubting him. I wondered if he was not really a Master. And, if it was indeed so, what should I do? Quit my discipleship, or simply consider whatever happens as part of my discipleship? But then, on the other hand, how could I know if this thought, or my every thought on this particular issue, was correct?

After many hours of doubt I eventually went to the Society with a feeling of great fatigue. I understood quite clearly that it originated from the conflict inside me and particularly from my doubts. But, no matter what I did, I could not chase them away, or rule on the soundness or not of my thoughts, nor give any answer on this matter myself; I could not even understand the reasons that had caused all this.

The Master's teaching seemed tiresome, clouding my mind even more, so I sat down to meditate as soon as I was alone. The fatigue and haze, although beginning to somewhat subside, still persisted. That was when the Master opened the door and approached me. Having realized what was happening to me, he advised me in a strict tone to stop dealing with frivolous matters. Nonsense he had called them, adding that I should immediately dismiss the ideas which had caused my distress.

But the issue had not cleared up inside me. The next day, I asked a disciple what he believed a Master was.

His answer did not satisfy me at the least. He said that he dare not even touch this concept; hardly an answer. In fact, I could discern his need to avoid a dialogue with himself. A dialogue that might put him on the spot, faced with the doubts he had been withholding. If there was something he truly did not dare, it was to confess to himself the thoughts he had been driving back. He was left to his silence and I to my thunderous thoughts...

It had only been a few days and I was aware that it was not possible to remain in this state. I had turned into a mobile source of negative thought transmissions for the Master. And, if nothing else, it was extremely paradoxical since I was called, and indeed I myself had chosen to express my true nature. And the true nature of each individual is at least free from such thought-forms. How could I convey to the other disciples, to my surroundings, and ultimately to all people, the clear current of love and interest, when I was in fact drowning in my own thoughts?

I talked to the Master about my doubts, my difficulty, my thoughts, as well as my decision to act. But my decision for action and realization would follow my own pace. The Master agreed. I felt relieved from the pressure tormenting me, but, strangely, another difficulty presented itself before me. I would be left on my own, relying solely on my own thoughts and distinctions. I was confronted with the acceptance that the Master had shown me, even if it was what I had asked of him. And so no peace or harmony came about. I continued to meditate, but as soon as something unpleasant came to mind, the fatigue would return.

Then came a moment of clarity. The clouds that prevented my sight stepped aside and I saw that I had to stop resisting my needs and difficulties. Their acceptance was what would lead me to the correct way of working, letting the delay take its course. The answer given to me through meditation was: "To express all that you meditate with love towards all." And I hoped that could happen without any other resistances and oppositions!

My wish did not come true. Not as I wanted it to, at least. And this no longer related to the mistrust I had previously expressed towards the Master, it did not concern the faults that suited me to accuse him of. My faith in him had recovered without doubts or hesitations. And when such a meaningless idea popped into my mind, instead of feeding it with emotional charges and thoughts on thoughts, I instantaneously chased it away. And, equally instantaneously, my confidence to the Master would return.

The problem was my own. And, although reduced, there were still times when it intensified. I meditated, I delved deep, looking for the solution, always based on the teaching. I wondered what I should do. No answer came, but even when I did receive one, it was not the one

I desired. And I repeated: "Question and no answer!" Was this also a lesson which I found difficulty in accepting?

It was only natural for my concern to lead me to the quest for the causes. Why when meditating did I not receive an answer every time, especially since it is always needed, whether a validation of the question, its correction, or even its rejection? A new meditation and new questions that were not answered. Suddenly, in an instant, I stopped desiring any answer. I realized that it would come only when and if the Entity decided to provide it. It knows everything that each of us is ready to accept and to realize. The Master does the same, sometimes validating, and other times rejecting a question, because he is united with the Entity.

What was given to me was plentiful and was consolidated every day through the discipleship, the meditations and their realization. And so I continued to work, always under the Entity's supervision.

But my stability in the supervision of the Entity was not manifested soon, but, on the contrary, was expressed very slowly. I knew there were still fears, resistances, cowardice and various other issues. Fortunately, I had accepted my voids so as to not become too agitated, as would happen previously whenever something unpleasant appeared.

The Master called me and told me the following: "Your discipleship in kindergarten has ended and you have begun your education in elementary school. Even if you are troubled when you make certain mistakes, you should consider them as exams preparing you to proceed further, to what is symbolically akin to a next class."

I agreed with everything he told me and with the de-symbolisation of the kindergarten and subsequent classes, which, if not for it, would have led to my collapse. The passage into adolescence that prepares for adulthood brings great pleasure to the human field. At the spiritual level, however, and since my discipleship began at the age of fifty, it was expected that I now began elementary school, what the Master called a first major initiation. He continued teaching me and I continued my discipleship with him.

THE FREEDOM OF UNION

I had already been with the Society for three years, and summer had come for good. It was around this time of the year when I had first come to the Society. During the two previous summers, I had barely visited our summer home. My need to constantly be in contact even with the Society's premises was great and, thus, equally great was the pressure I felt when I was absent. The simplicity, however, with which I functioned for the first time that summer, going without difficulty to the countryside for rest, was due to a – partial even – realization of the teaching which hitherto still seemed as a wonderful theory.

The teaching had been watering me, initiating the production of the awareness in the uniformity of all things and situations, as the Master had told us. His words had begun bearing fruit within me – the increasing union with my true nature validated in me the common identity of the Society's areas with any other premise, such as that of our summer home. Through the acceptance of the hidden consubstantial, I could equate all things; my house, my neighbourhood, my city, the country, the continent, the planet, the entire world. The concept of space did not limit or bound me anymore and the specific location of our summer home, away from the Society, ceased being a red cloth to me. On the contrary, it calmed and pleased me. So, for the first time, having already been adequately covered by the teaching, I went with simplicity to the countryside.

"The essence is everywhere, in the Society, in Athens, in Greece, in Europe, in the countries of the continents. This realization is requested of the disciples by the Masters."

His words were expected to raise the need for further confirmation that this essence for which our Master spoke of was literally everywhere, in the mountains, the seas, the sky, the atmosphere. His answer was affirmative. Yes, this essence is within everything. But what if I closed myself up in my room with secured windows and a locked door? That was the naive question one of us asked him.

The Master smiled at the question. He explained that the essence permeates everything and not just those relating to nature. All that is artificial and constructed by humans, such as walls and doors, are permeated by the essence. Besides, he added, these are also parts of nature as they are manufactured by its materials.

Some of us fell in contemplation. The Master asked them why and what they thought of. After a while, one disciple asked hesitantly:

"Why is it that when we are alone in a room we feel lonely?"

"Because you do not yet experience the essence of yourself, your true nature, and limit it to only a few things that lead you, albeit briefly, in ignorance of its existence. Meditate regularly in order to realize its ubiquitous presence more and more."

After the questions and analyses, I decided to rid myself of any identification, seeking as always the support of the spiritual field.

I was walking on the street. I do not remember much of that time, not even the time or what I was thinking during those moments. But what I clearly remember is the image of a man I saw – a man who seemed tormented by great psychological difficulties. He avoided even looking at passers-by and I thought that he probably did not even want to hear them. Because of his difficulties, he seemed as though he sought isolation, something which prevented him from uniting with others around him.

When I eventually got home, I sat on the balcony and contemplated on the many difficulties people have. I looked at passers-by and unwittingly noticed many who walked slowly as if dragging their selves with difficulty, or as if dragging a burden behind them. And yet, many of them were young people. What was really tormenting them? What did they feel and why were they suffering? Of course I did not know the specific reason for each person, nor could I learn it. But, it was obvious that something was at fault, something that burdened them and made things difficult for them, such as fear, anxiety or difficulty in resolving a problem.

All I wanted was to dispel any obstacle, any barrier between us and unite with those people, all people, acquaintances and strangers. I realized that only then is true freedom and union experienced, and not only during a meditation. The true union is within the daily happenings, through life, and only there can it be entirely realized by us. The realization of the union is here and now, throughout all of the day's hours.

THE MASTER WITHIN ME

My discipleship was not without insecurities and resistances. One day, as soon as I started meditating, I
began feeling really bad. I identified with my retentions,
but also with the idea of the oppression that I believed I
had been receiving from others.

When I went to the Society, I asked the Master why
this had happened and why I had felt so bad, and especially at the moment when I had just begun meditating.

"Because you still consider the Master as a prop, and
place him opposite you," he replied unexpectedly. "But
the Master is within you."

I decided to activate myself. As I projected my concern for others even more dynamically, the retention and oppression dissolved. For the first time after two years of discipleship, I had realized that in order to be free I should stop needing any prop or other dependency. The Master taught me to rely on the Master within me, not on himself. But who was this Master within me with whom I had not yet been introduced? He was exactly the same as the Society's Master, whom I could see and touch, whose presence was manifested even in my dreams, or through them; he was the supervisor of my course, the difficulty that would appear, and at the same time my succourer! He was a broad consciousness field!

I started thinking about the people of my surroundings. How many of them were self-sufficient and functioned self-reliantly? And how many were those who cheated themselves and erroneously imagined something like that for themselves? Of all friends or relatives, I focused on the one I knew best – my husband. I wondered if the confidence he showed was fictitious, a projection of his own that served his need to appear independent and autonomous. Or was it indeed faith in himself and the fact that he stood on his own legs without crutches and props? His need for recognition from others, the narrations of all his accomplishments to acquaintances, his perseverance in thoroughly dealing with anything he addressed, even with our children's model kits when they were young, seemed to belie the purity of confidence in himself. He had accomplished much in his life and I admired him for it, but, just like the rest of us, he sought the reward, verbal or other, of others. This dependence of ours on the opinion of others turns their kind words into our prop. Our society is structured on interdependent relationships, relationships that at the same time act competitively – as a prop; on emotional relationships with their ups and downs, where each party is engaged in the search for their own right and the blaming of responsibilities on others.

The love of my husband for us – for myself, our children and all the people close to him – was undeniable. But his love, his interest, was confined to the circle of his family and friends. His interest in the progress of society was obvious, but where was the true love for each and every human in the world? As a disciple that I was, I was called to express this love. And through this steady position for others would also come the change in them. Expressing, for example, my adoration for my husband, I would help ensure that, at his own pace, he would break his bonds and spread his interest to more and more people. This was the capability I had and this was my strength. And the more I became a prop for others, the more exempt I became of the need to have a prop myself. And without a prop I became even more substantially free and able to convey with patience and understanding the teaching, responding to my fellow humans, who in turn, covered by the love they had received, would respond to the same request of others.

LIFE AND DEATH

Surprisingly, I had been neglecting to talk to the Master from the start about something that had been bothering me for quite some time. Only when it happened again towards the end of the first year of my discipleship did I decide to mention it to him. For several years before my discipleship began, there were times when my husband seemed to be immersed in unpleasant thoughts, remaining lost in them for hours. I asked him about it, but most times he would not even respond to my questions, so intense was his absorption. Only a few times did he talk to me about the occupation period, without however explaining anything to me in detail. I knew a few minor things, but, as I was unable to help him, he soon returned to his tormented state.

The Master had met my husband, as he had accompanied me to the Society at times, and had expressed an interest in him as well as his work. What the Master told me about the conditions of the occupation and how it had affected my husband, as well as many others of our compatriots, were neither unheard of before nor unseen. The occupation had affected everyone who had lived through it, especially the soldiers and those who were members of the resistance. And I am certain that those of you that are younger have heard stories and tales of those difficult times from the older generations. Nothing guaranteed the next day or even the next moment – fear and anguish prevailed. The Master once again praised the stance and the power put forward by Greece during the Second World War.

From my husband's half-spoken words, which I passed on to the Master, it was clear that he had been actively involved in the war and had experienced its atrocities up close. It was not at all surprising that he had been carrying the burden of those images inside of him; images of horror and death. Yes, I was aware of all this, the Master was not telling me anything new. But his manner – that was the difference. The current that spread around us as I discussed with him, his caring, his great embrace that could hold everything, the power he conveyed, the purity of the Higher Intellect through which all events of life are filtered, even the sound of his voice, had the ability to dissolve any darkness that had spread its nets in our hearts and minds. Besides, these experiences became the springboard for writing this particular book, attempting to capture as best I could his adoration towards everyone and everything; not the teaching, his analyses and meditative regimens that I routinely attempted to write down in my previous books, and for which anyone could easily refer me to the sayings of other wise men throughout the ages. This was my Master – the one who committed himself to my evolution and took me by the hand as a schoolgirl and led me safely and under his protection on the long road towards union with the Self!

The conversation with him reassured me greatly. At last I deeply and accurately understood my husband's difficulty, along with its cause. I continued performing spiritual healing on him until completely eliminating his unpleasant thoughts. Moreover, I realized that part of the fatigue I had since the time I still worked, before meeting the Master, came, without my being aware of it, from my husband's heavy disposition that, as expected, affected me negatively.

One day, a friend of my husband's came to visit. After welcoming him and offering him something to drink, I sat down to join them. We discussed various things until he mentioned a vision of his in which he saw himself as a perfect human being. He was represented with a large radiative power, with superpowers and survivability through very dangerous circumstances and situations which steeled his resolution to remain in this dynamic function. I did not partake in this particular conversation, only silently listened and thought. In his vision certain negative elements lurked, but I did not share my thoughts with them. I preferred to examine on my own the doubts I had concerning the vision he had recounted.

When he left our house and my husband proceeded to occupy himself with his projects, the necessary conditions of quiet ensued, letting me deal with the analysis of his vision. I reasonably and spontaneously wondered about what his visions would offer to the human existence. Resilience and survival skills in difficult situations were accompanied by the risk of complacency. It is our shortcomings that inevitably turn us towards the inner field and the teaching. It is the difficulties that become the driving force in the conquest of wider consciousness fields and it is these that urge us to the emergence of positive aspects and the assimilation of the negative with the agatho*.

Superpowers were never what we asked for, especially when used for personal gain. The responsibility of power must always be accompanied by offering, which not by

---

*The term "agatho" out of the Greek word 'αγαθό' is used to mean all that is beyond the duality of good and bad. It is the Entity, the Whole, the Monad.

accident is also what super-hero films illustrate. Besides, we all possess a superpower, yet we let it fall into disuse; the superpower of love. The being is perfected by the stable expression of its true nature, and, in this case, supernatural powers are of little significance.

It had been ten years since I had begun my discipleship and my husband all of a sudden fell ill. At the hospital he was diagnosed with pulmonary oedema and he passed away soon after. My son took care of the burial details, and we returned home. No matter what my children told me in consolation, my pain was just too great. The phone calls from disciples, relatives and acquaintances did not stop. My pain softened up slightly when talking to them, but as soon as I put down the handset, deep sadness came back and I would start crying again.

When the Master called me, he told me that it was only natural to hurt for the loss of my husband. He liberated me by telling me to let myself cry as long as I needed, even in front of others or outside of our home.

The Master continued to call me again and again, and slowly, with his words and with the current that he conveyed to me, I started feeling reassured that my husband's soul would always be well. The discipleship I received at that time was very important. It helped me to steadily seek the experience of my true nature.

The loneliness I felt was immense. Our children were now adults and had long since moved out, so the house was now empty. I had no company, no one to go for a walk with, to have a conversation with or to care for in times of need. The feeling of loneliness that I felt expanded so much that it eventually turned to futility towards the world. There came moments when I asked his soul: "Why did you leave me? What will I do now that you are no longer with me?"

The great pain over the loss of my husband lasted a month and a half, until I gradually began adapting to a life without him. I began writing books again, I continued with the groups I had taken on at the Society and I worked for spiritual healing, always under the Master's guidance. Only after some time did the Master gently admonish me on the manner in which I had been dealing with my husband's death. I accepted his words and realized that in doing so he aided me in placing myself correctly towards his passing and move away from the sadness. Everything he told me was aimed at one thing: love and service to all.

Over time, my thoughts on the death of my husband began to fade. I realized now that by not clinging to his memory I allowed my own soul to calm. Whenever the sadness returned, the harder and with more love would I surrender myself to the expression of the soul's current, and the feelings in me would subside.

Our life, from the moment of our birth until our death, is a discipleship. A constant, endless and diverse discipleship. In this position we must face our life and it is a conscious passage that changes everything and transforms all.

EPILOGUE

The work of the Master did not stop at any obstacle. Even when he was ill, I would go to his house and he would dictate texts to me. His poems, as well as the analyses he made of other writers' poems aided me in better understanding his teaching.

When I was at his home I realized how often he received phone calls from his disciples. He would stop focusing on writing and deal with them and whatever they told him. He spoke to them as much as was needed, regardless of the discussion's length, and this would be repeated over and over. For me, this was further validation of the work and nature of the Master.

The years passed as if by magic, until something happened that shocked us greatly: the Master had cancer. It was the third time it had appeared in his lifetime. His disciples performed spiritual healing on him in the faith that he would be cured. I continued going to his home and he continued telling me what to write. He called his disciples and encouraged them to come by his house whenever they had a problem, even though his illness was not cured.

What was all this he did? Was it not an ultimate expression of his work? Was it not a continuous stability in its realization? This is what creates awe towards the Master and all Masters. They strengthen the will of the disciples to follow their course and convey it to all people. There is no solution other than this, the only reality, which leads us to the essence of ourselves.

The Master passed away on October 21, 1995. It was a Saturday at seven o' clock in the morning. All disciples went to his house, before going to his funeral, and we were all greatly saddened, while some cried for his loss. In the face of the Master I noticed an expression of power and love; the same that he always steadily had towards us. I bid him farewell with a short speech. I spoke of his work and his complete personality that always expressed interest and love for all. My belief was that he would continue to do so even after his death.

After the end of the funeral, the disciples, including myself, went to the Society. We stayed there until late at night. As soon as I returned home I meditated and I received a message from the Master.

"Accept the spiritual field within you completely, radiate it and spread it to others."

A circle had closed, another had just opened. The Master's death in no way marked the end of our discipleship or the termination of the Society's work. We had to continue without his physical presence, but with his essence present always and everywhere. We were called to responsibly realize his work, utilizing the teaching he had provided to us and would continue to provide steadily thenceforth, and to convey it to the members of the Society and to all people. This responsibility would strengthen even more our union with the Master and what he had taught us and continued doing for those seeking to receive his teaching.

"Even if only one disciple is consolidated in the teaching received, it will help other disciples to also be gradually consolidated by implementing what I have taught them and still continue to do," the Master once said.

A year after his death, Kiki Keramida, who was responsible for guiding the members who wanted to become spiritual healers, also passed away. The void of her absence had to be covered, and I took it upon myself to continue their training.

One of the basic principles of spiritual healing is the awareness that it is carried out by the Entity. The healers express Its work as pure conduits through their union with It. And they learn to become conduits of this radiance that surrounds us everywhere and constantly. In other words, the disciple is by definition a healer and functions in a healing manner not only during a healing in the strict sense of the term, but constantly, within the entire spectrum of life.

The realization of the teaching, beyond its beneficial effects, was the tangible proof that this was a workable knowledge and not an abstract theory. And it was practical and workable in the significant aspects of life equally as in those that seemed small, in the daily difficulties and situations that many people considered insignificant; my interest in my respective interlocutor, the care of my husband's needs as well as many more, were the daily realizations of the teaching, whose achievement was easy and direct, as the Master never neglected to point out. And so I always, to the extent that anyone was ready to understand, conveyed the teaching, either with words or with my actions or with my life example.

The processes for the path I followed next to the Master had already begun from when I first met him, if not much earlier, since all previous events of my life probably aimed at this alone. At that time I was not able to attribute the extent of his love, nor define the meaning of the Entity But, this knowledge became necessary for the path I wished to realize, regardless of the difficulties and resistances I encountered. My will to constantly march on grew stronger by the day, reducing the ignorance and reactions to their final demise. With the same strong will I still continue along my path.

Klairi Lykiardopoulou

Klairi Lykiardopoulou was born in Athens. She went to school at the American College and completed her studies in pedagogy in the United States.

In 1980 she became member of Omilos Eksipiretiton - the "Servers' Society" Spiritual Centre and received teachings on self-study and the emergence of the spiritual nature of man with the guidance of its founder, Dimitris Kakalidis. For almost three decades, she was President of the Society and was dedicated to its task.

She wrote 19 books, conveying her personal experiences and the knowledge she acquired from the teaching of the Servers' Society, with an aim to demonstrate a dynamic way of life and a philosophical view which can help people to solve their problems when applied.

For her literary work she has recieved commending reviews by the country's intellectual world. Extracts of her books have been included in anthologies and literary magazines. Her trilogy about the role of man, woman and the couple was approved for school libraries.

She passed away in 2015, leaving a great legacy to all who continue the Society's work.

MEGAS SEIRIOS PUBLICATIONS
English Editions

The Concealed Lotus of Manifestation
Fallen Paradise Holy Matter
Logos the Third
a poetic trilogy by Dimitris Kakalidis (bilingual edition)

Incentives I & Incentives II
poetic collections by Dimitris Kakalidis (bilingual edition)

The Revelation of the Entity
by Dimitris Kakalidis

The Wisdom of the Poem
by Dimitris Kakalidis

Spiritual Healing,
A human potential in theory and practice
by Klairi Lykiardopoulou

The Master [1],
First Concepts – First Experiences
by Klairi Lykiardopoulou

The Path from Fear to Fearlessness
by Ioanna Dimakou

Individuality Unity Monad
by Klairi Lykiardopoulou

Seeking... from Alpha to Omega,
Synthesis of Science and Philosophy
by Mina Gouvatsou-Karekou

I Will be Here (poetry)
by Paraskevi Kostopetrou

• **Small Temples on a Wave** (poetry)
• **Fiery Notion** (poetry)
by Vassiliki Ergazaki

Experiences of a Spiritual Healer
by Kiki Keramida

...And the Shadows Became Light
by Klairi Lykiardopoulou

You can Open Your Eyes Now
by Ade Durojaiye

Greek Editions

Dimitris Kakalidis
- The Wisdom of the Poem
- The Wisdom of the Short Story

Poetic Trilogy:
- The Hidden Lotus of Revelation
- Fallen Paradise Holy Matter
- Logos the Third

Poetic Collection:
- Incentives I
- Incentives II

- The Revelation of the Entity

Klairi Lykiardopoulou
- Woman - Exploring her Position and Role in Society
- Man - Exploring his Position and Role in Society
- Couple - Exploring its Position and Role in Society
- Spiritual Healing, *A human potential in theory and practice*
- The Master [1], *First Concepts – First Experiences*
- The Master [2], *The Awakening of the Soul*
- The Master [3], *Processes of the Mind*
- The Master [4], *Accomplishment – Spiritual Healing*
- The Knowledge of the Educator
- The Power of the Woman
- Man and Money, *A philosophical study of their relationship*
- Individuality Unity Monad
- The Family Circle
- The Sacred Task of the Soul
- The Heart of the Earth, *Imaginary Short-stories to give Light to our Planet!*
- The Diachronic Master [1], *Seeking the Knowledge in simple thoughts and deeds*
- The Diachronic Master [2], *Discipleship in the Eternal Truths*
- The Diachronic Master [3], *The Power of Love*
- The Diachronic Master [4], *Our Hidden and Apparent Self*
- ... And the Shadows became Light

Dimitris Karvounis – Dimitris Kakalidis
Alalum and Hallelujah (poetry)

Dimitris Karvounis
- The Crypt and the Nest (and other stories)
- Lilian
- My Spirit Crucified (poetry)
- The Eternally Collected (poetry)

Ninon Dimitriadou-Kampouri
Fear Not, Day is Breaking! (poetry)

Ioanna Dimakou
The Path from Fear to Fearlessness

Kiki Keramida
Experiences of a Spiritual Healer

Petros Panteloglou
The Road I Chose
A Professional Driver's Path to Spirituality

Mina Gouvatsou-Karekou
Seeking... from Alpha to Omega
A Synthesis of Science and Philosophy

Vassiliki K. Ergazaki
- Small Temples on a Wave (poetry)
- Fiery Notion (poetry)
- For the Flowers to Sing (poetry)

Dionisis Dimakos
Flows of Reflection and Heart (poetry)

Paraskevi Kostopetrou
I Will be Here (poetry)

Ade Durojaiye
You Can Open Your Eyes Now

www.ingramcontent.com/pod-product-compliance
Lightning Source LLC
Chambersburg PA
CBHW051716090426
42738CB00010B/1940